RUISLIP PAST

First published 1994
by Historical Publications Ltd
32 Ellington Street, London N7 8PL
(Telephone 071-607 1628)

ISBN 0 948667 29 X
British Library Cataloguing-in-Publication Data.
A catalogue record for this book is available from the British Library.

Typeset by Historical Publications Ltd
Printed in Zaragoza, Spain by
Edelvives

RUISLIP PAST

A Visual History
of Ruislip
Eastcote and Northwood

by Eileen M. Bowlt

HISTORICAL PUBLICATIONS

Acknowledgements

No local historian can uncover the history of a specific place without the help of librarians and archivists and older residents. I should like to thank the staff at Ruislip Library, the Heritage Team at Uxbrige Library; the archivists of King's College, Cambridge, St George's Windsor and the Greater London Record Office; the vicar and churchwardens of St Martin's, Ruislip, and the headteachers of local schools; all of whom have made documents available to me.

Residents who have talked to me about life in Ruislip before it was a suburb, especially Miss Rene Twitchen and Mrs Alice Hood (who watched the railway lines being laid and the building of Ruislip Station), Mr Ian Tait and the late Stanley and Helen Hoare, have brought the years of Ruislip's transition from a farming community to a London suburb alive for me.

Discussions with members of my Extra-Mural classes and the Research Group of the Ruislip, Northwood & Eastcote Local History Society have helped me to clarify my thoughts on some of the more obscure aspects of Ruislip's past.

Finally, I should like to thank my husband Colin who has always supported my researches and helped with the proof-reading and indexing of this book.

The Illustrations

With the exception of those noted below, all the illustrations were supplied and are reproduced with the kind permission of Hillingdon Heritage Services. Others are are reproduced with the permission of the following:

Eileen M. Bowlt *23, 24, 25, 28, 29, 31, 51, 53, 59, 74, 86, 142, 143, 159*
British Library: *42*
Dennis Edwards: *124*
National Monuments Record: *35, 172*
Martin Pym: *48, 49, 62*
Uxbridge Gazette: *163, 164, 166, 167, 174*

Contents

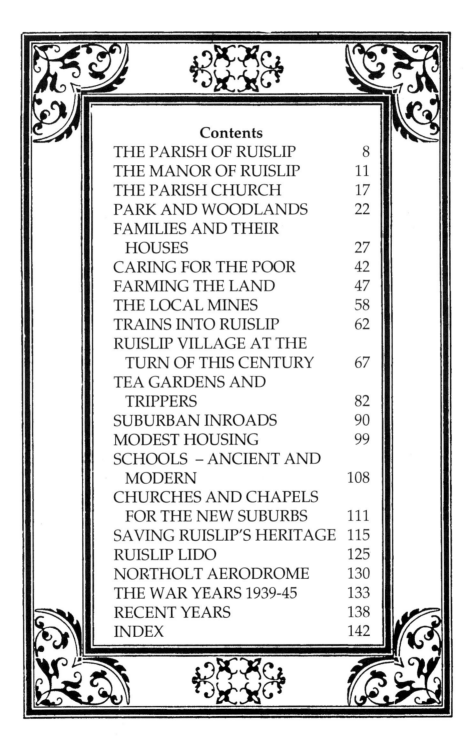

Further Reading

BOWLT C. & Eileen M. — *The History and Natural History of Ruislip Woods.* Ruislip, Northwood & Eastcote Local History Society, 1982.

BOWLT Eileen M. — *The Goodliest Place in Middlesex.* Hillingdon Borough Libraries, 1989. (ISBN 0 907869 11 4)

COX Colleen A. — *A Quiet and Secluded Spot.* Ruislip, Northwood & Eastcote Local History Society, 1991. (ISBN 0 9507154 3 3)

EDWARDS R. — *Eastcote from Village to Suburb.* Hillingdon Borough Libraries, 1987. (ISBN 0 907869 09 2)

KEMP W.A.G. — *The Story of Northwood and Northwood Hills.* RNELHS Reprint, 1982

KEMP W.A.G. — *The History of Eastcote*, 1963.

MORRIS L.E. — *A History of Ruislip.* Ruislip Residents' Association, 1956.

TOTTMAN David — *Ruislip-Northwood. An early example of Town Planning.* RNELHS, 1982.

All the above are available at Hillingdon Borough Libraries.

Introduction

Ruislip is the sort of place which many people are surprised to find has a history; and if by history is meant the story of battles, famous people and great events, they are justified. No military conflicts took place in the parish and even the tide of the Civil War came no closer than Uxbridge, but Lady Bankes who so stoutly defended Corfe Castle against the Roundheads was born at Eastcote House and is buried at St Martin's, and others of more than local repute have resided in the area in more recent times. Jeffrey Farnol, the historical novelist, lived at 3 King's End and Dr Christopher Addison, the first Minister of Health, at 'Pretty Corner', Northwood, for instance.

To go back in time, Ruislip was second only to Hayes in the Hundred of Elthorne, both in size and value, at the time of the Domesday Book and probably had a motte-bailey castle for a short time after the Conquest. During the overlordship of the Abbey of Bec (1087-1414) Ruislip was important as one of the most productive manors and as the place where the central audit of all Bec's English properties was held. The Great Barn, the finest of the buildings at Manor Farm, is a legacy of that period, as are court rolls and a customal which draw aside the veil that hides the lives of our forebears and gives us tantalising glimpses of their duties, peccadilloes and interests.

The ancient parish and manor of Ruislip covered the whole of modern Ruislip, Northwood and Eastcote. Until the coming of the Metropolitan Railway to Northwood in 1887 most of the farms and cottages were in Westcote (Ruislip) and Eastcote, with only a handful lying north of the great belt of woodland, much of which survives. Practically everyone was involved in agriculture, with a few brick and tile makers and chalk and sand miners at various times, and the usual village craftsmen and traders.

King's College, Cambridge, lords of the manor from 1451 to the 20th century, had a very large demesne (land retained by the lord and worked by his servants) running from Northwood through Copse and Park Woods, Manor Farm and south to the Yeading Brook. A number of other estates based on large houses grew, especially in the 19th century. The opening of the various railway stations from 1887-1908 led to the selling of these properties for house building and the development of the suburbs of Ruislip, Northwood and Eastcote. The fact that their layout is on Garden Suburb lines is due to the energy and far-sightedness of Edmund Abbott, Frank Elgood and other members of the newly-formed Urban District Council, who promoted a Town Planning Scheme as early as 1910.

Between the time when the countryside was first opened up to Londoners in the late 1880s and the disappearance of the fields and country lanes in the late 1920s, the whole area enjoyed a period of fame as a rural retreat and place of resort for day-trippers. Tea gardens abounded.

This book recounts the high spots of Ruislip's history from the time of the Domesday Book to the late 20th century with the aid of numerous pictures. Details left out of the explanatory text may be found in the books and articles mentioned in the Further Reading list.

Eileen M. Bowlt

The Parish of Ruislip

The ancient parish of Ruislip lies towards the north-west corner of the county of Middlesex, within the hundred of Elthorne. Its northern boundary is the shire ditch that runs along the edge of Batchworth Heath, dividing Middlesex from Hertfordshire and its eastern edge marches with that of Elthorne. Today the hundreds into which counties were divided in Saxon times are almost forgotten and the suburbs of Ruislip, Northwood and Eastcote, which now cover the old parish, are part of the Borough of Hillingdon.

THE MEANING OF RUISLIP

The name has been spelt in at least sixty different ways over the centuries. Its earliest form, in the Domesday Book, is 'Rislepe'. Later it appears with a 'u' instead of an 'i', as Russelep and Rushlep and many other variations, which have led to the supposition that it should still be pronounced that way. Indeed people with long memories insist that it was called 'Ruselip' although spelt in the modern way, in their youth. At the beginning of the 19th century official documents like the Enclosure Award were headed 'Ruislip alias Riselip'.

Ekwall in the *Concise Oxford Dictionary of English Place Names* suggests that the elements of the name are the Old English 'rysc' meaning rush and 'slaep', a wet place, but points out that the second element might be 'hlype' which translates as leap. So whether Ruislip means a wet place where the rushes grow or a rushy leap is open to question, but in either case the name probably arose from its establishment near the marshy banks of the Pinn.

EARLIEST RUISLIP

The Domesday Book describes Ruislip as a manor, but as one of the inhabitants was a priest, there was probably already a parish church. The Norman lord was Ernulf de Hesdin and Ruislip had belonged to a Saxon, Wlward Wit in the time of King Edward. The neighbouring manors of Harefield and Northolt had priests in residence as well, but nearby Ickenham, part of which had also been in the ownership of Wlward Wit, had not. Perhaps he had installed the priest to serve all his people in the neighbourhood.

Archaeological digs and chance finds have not yet provided any evidence of continuous settlement in

1. The Domesday Book entry for Rislepe (Ruislip) under the heading 'The lands of Ernulf de Hesding in Helethorn Hundred'.

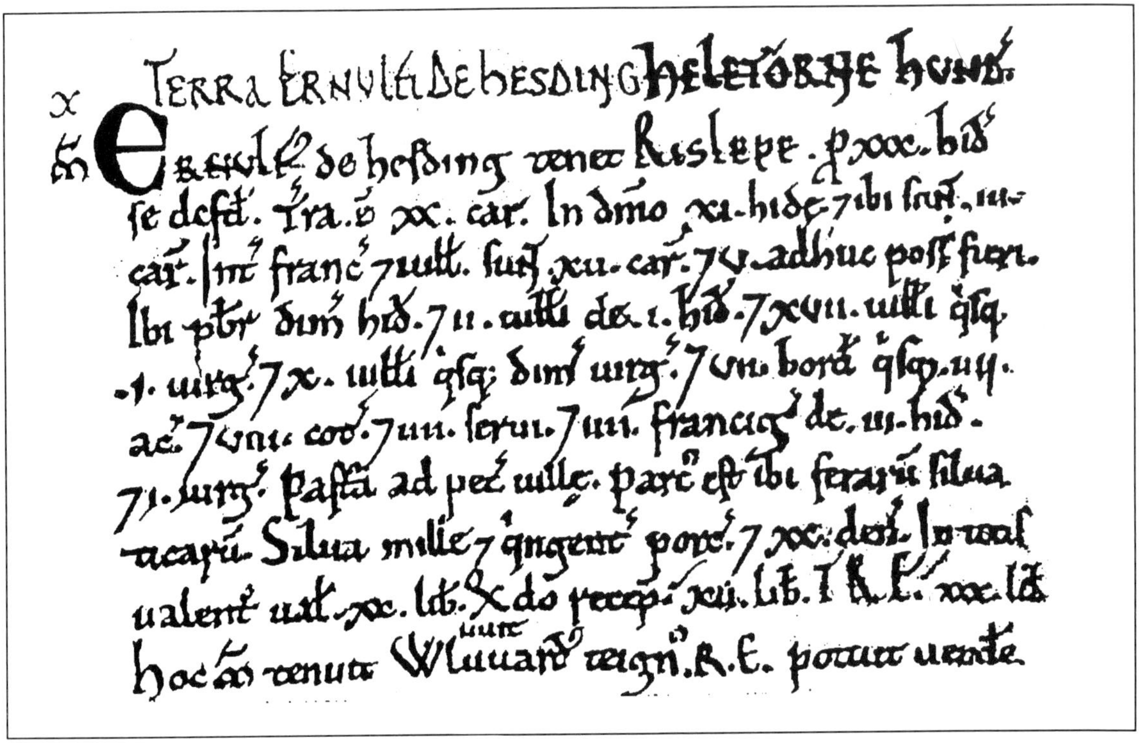
TERRA ERNULFI DE HESDING Helethorne hund.
Ernulf de hesding ten Rislepe. p xxx. hid
se defd. Tra. e xx. car. In dnio xi. hide 7 ibi sunt. iii.
car. Int franc 7 uitt. sunt. xii. car. 7 v. adhuc poss fieri.
Ibi pbr dim hid. 7 ii. uitti de. i. hid. 7 xvii. uitti qsq.
i. uirg. 7 x. uitti qsq; dim uirg. 7 vii. bord qsq. iiii.
ac. 7 viii. cot. 7 iiii. serui. 7 iiii. francig de. iii. hid.
7 i. uirg. Pasta ad pec uillae. Parc e ibi ferarum silua
ticarum. Silua mille 7 qngent porc. 7 xx. den. In tot
ualent uat. xx. lib. X do recep: xii. lib. T.R.E. xxx. lib.
Hoc .M. tenuit Wluuard uuit teign. R.E. potuit uendere.

2. *The Parish of Riselip (Ruislip) as depicted in Rocque's map of the county of Middlesex dated 1754.*

the Ruislip area before late Saxon times. Flint flakes, scrapers, arrow heads and knives dating from the mesolithic and neolithic periods and the Bronze Age have turned up in gardens along the valley of the Pinn and in Park Wood in recent years and probably indicate settlement in the alluvial deposits of the river, perhaps made by migrants from the more densely populated Colne Valley. Small quantities of Roman material have been found around Manor Farm.

The reason for the lack of signs of habitation may be the woodland on the northern uplands of the parish, shown on Rocque's 1754 map and still fairly extensive today (600 acres), which is believed to be the remnant of the forest which once covered much of Middlesex. Clearance necessary for growing crops would be easier in the lowland parts of the county to the south, where settlement is apparent in earlier Saxon times and where the brickearths were easier to cultivate than the heavy clay soils found north of the line of the Uxbridge Road.

RUISLIP AT DOMESDAY

The Domesday Book description of Ruislip unfolds a picture of a heavily wooded landscape (enough woodland to support 1500 pigs), with much arable land (sufficient for 20 ploughs) and pasture for the village livestock. An interesting feature as there was only one other mentioned in Middlesex, was a park for woodland beasts. Traces of the boundary banks can still be seen in Park Wood.

Most of the 53 people mentioned were presumably heads of households, so the population was probably a little under 250. It included four Frenchmen who may have been officials of some kind and four slaves who would have lived in other people's houses, perhaps in the lord's hall. There were 29 villeins who, at that time, probably held their land freely from the lord in return for both rent and labour services. By the 12th or 13th centuries villeins had become unfree, though not necessarily poor men tied to their lords. The seven bordars were probably smallholders, with a cottage and about 5 acres of land, while the eight cottars were similar in status, but with rather less land.

Since the county and hundred boundaries predate the Conquest and are unlikely to have changed and as the bordering vills of Harefield, Ickenham and Northolt are also mentioned in the Domesday Book, it seems reasonable to assume that Ruislip in 1086 covered the same area as the 20th-century Ruislip-Northwood Urban District – about 6500 acres. In 1991 the population was 70,426.

LAND USE AND SETTLEMENT PATTERN

The pattern of land use already established by 1086 of woodland to the north, arable land to the south and pasture and meadow along the three main streams, the Pinn, the Yeading and the Roxbourne, persisted until modern times. Rocque's map shows the medieval open fields in their 18th century form, but unfortunately only names some of them and uses his own idiosyncratic spelling.

Running east from the church where the word 'Riselip' appears on the map were three fields, Church Field, Gt Windmill Field and Lt Windmill Field. The words 'Riselip Field' lie across Marlpit Field and Stene Field. Bone Field is actually Bourne Field. Aldeston Field is an 18th-century name for Tybber Field and the two unnamed fields to the south of it are Hill Field and Whittingrove Field. Across the southern edge of the parish ran fields called Roxbourne. Priors Field and Ascott Bushes are enclosures within one of them. Above Ascott Bushes lay Well Field and East Field ran down the eastern boundary of the parish.

The houses were scattered in small hamlets near the church, at the field ends and along the lanes leading up to the common woodland which lay beyond the Park.

WESTCOTE, EASTCOTE AND NORTHWOOD

By the middle of the 13th century Ruislip was divided into three tithings, Westcote, Ascot (Eastcote) and Norwood (Northwood). All male landowners over 12 years of age were supposed to be in a tithing and the members were mutually responsible for good behaviour. The names of the tithings represent a western settlement, an eastern settlement and one north of the woods. Westcote having the church and lord's hall was probably the earliest of the three to become established. The open fields were divided between Westcote and Eastcote by a ridgeway which can be traced today for much of its length in a modern footpath. Stene Field, Well Field, one of the Roxbournes and East Field were in Eastcote.

Northwood always differed from the other two vills. An outpost of the manor was built there in the 13th century and land seems to have been cleared from the woodland for cultivation, but no open fields were created. Six ploughmen lived at the manorial grange in Northwood in 1324, servants of the lord, which suggests that the arable was part of the demesne (lord's land). Down in Westcote and Eastcote, the central portion of the open fields were kept in demesne, but on either side the people who lived in the cottages had strips of land.

For administrative purposes in the 17th, 18th and early 19th centuries Westcote and Eastcote were still treated separately, each having a constable and an overseer of the poor, who kept their own accounts. Northwood was shared geographically between the two. This division was discontinued in Jan 1833, being considered 'useless and unnecessary' by the Vestry.

The Manor of Ruislip

WLWARD WIT AND ERNULF DE HESDIN

The lords of Ruislip have never been simple country gentlemen. Wlward Wit was one of Edward the Confessor's thanes and had land in eleven counties, most of which he lost at the Conquest. Ernulf de Hesdin succeeded to many of his properties, including Ruislip and Kingsbury in the county of Middlesex. Two medieval chronicles say that he died in the Holy Land. William of Malmesbury asserts that he made a pilgrimage to Jerusalem in thanksgiving after having had his paralysed hands cured by balm from the tomb of St Aldhelm, but the Book of the Monastery of Hyde recorded that he joined Duke Robert's crusade in 1095 to escape the king's wrath, having been wrongfully accused of being implicated in a plot to replace William Rufus on the throne with Stephen of Aumale and died before the walls of Antioch. In late 20th-century Ruislip his name is commemorated in the Hesdin Hall on Pembroke Road and in June each year masses are said for the repose of his soul, one at the Sacred Heart church and the other on the motte at Manor Farm by the Vicar of Ruislip.

Some years before he left England, probably in the spring of 1087, he granted Ruislip to the Abbey of Bec in Normandy. The charter of confirmation dated September 1087 specifically excluded a portion of Ruislip which was held by the Abbey of Holy Trinity at Rouen. The land in question was a tract of wooded waste lying on the west side of Bury Street and Ducks Hill, now Mad Bess Wood and land to the south, known at different times as St Catherine's Manor, the Little Manor or Katherine's End. One of the suburban streets in that area is called St Catherine's Road. The name comes from the fact that Holy Trinity held relics of that saint. The main manor of Ruislip remained in the care of the Abbey of Bec for more than 300 years.

THE LORD'S HALL

The moated area at Manor Farm is an ancient monument, scheduled as a motte-bailey castle. There is certainly an artificial mound partially encircled by a waterlogged moat, but it is not very high and has never been officially investigated by archaeologists. The circular moat was extended northwards to surround a bailey or courtyard, forming an oval enclosure in which the early 16th century Manor Farmhouse still stands. That part of the moat was filled in

3. The moat around the motte at Manor Farm, photographed in 1932. The hayricks stand on what is now the bowling green.

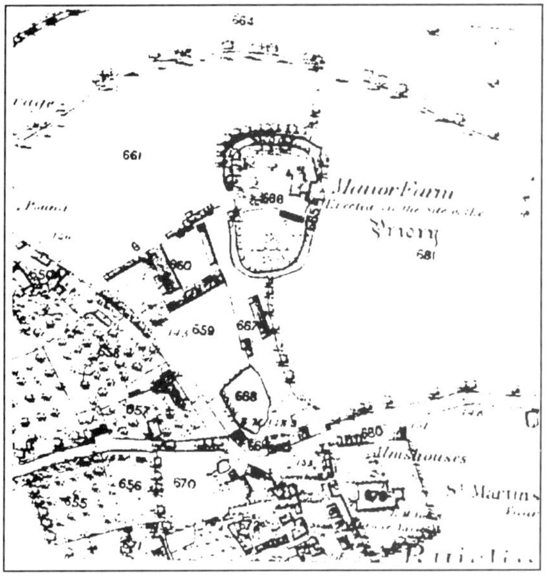

4. A portion of the 1865 Ordnance Survey map showing the complete moat around Manor Farm and the ditch to the north, which may have formed part of a village earthwork.

by Henry James Ewer who farmed Manor farm, in 1888, but its position can clearly be seen as a dip in the ground. The shape of the moats indicate an 11th century date and a fortified building of some sort. Moreover the site is at the bottom of Bury Street, a name which can mean fortification.

The motte may have been begun and abandoned, but if a castle was built the work must have been begun soon after 1066 and it must have ceased to be a castle before 1086, otherwise it would have been mentioned in the Domesday Book. The value of Ruislip declined from £30 in the time of King Edward to only £12 when it was handed over to Ernulf de Hesdin, which suggests that it was ravaged in some way, perhaps being stripped of its crops by a column of the Norman army. A strong building may then have become necessary to subdue a hostile population.

THE ABBEY OF BEC

The great Benedictine Abbey of Bec was founded by Herlwyn at the confluence of the Bec and Risle rivers in Normandy in 1040 and quickly became renowned for its spiritual and intellectual life. Many of William the Conqueror's followers endowed it with English lands scattered across the southern counties. Small cells were established on the manors where one or two monks lived and administered the estates. There was certainly one at Ruislip by the 12th century.

During the 13th century 24 of Bec's manors were grouped into the Bailiwick of Ogbourne and administered by two priories, one at Ogbourne in Wiltshire, the other at Ruislip, where the Proctor-General seems to have lived. For the next 150 years Ruislip enjoyed an importance it has never had since, as the central audit of the English lands was certainly held there. The common lordship united the widespread manors as the officials moved from one to the other, holding courts and transacting business. The ordinary people of Ruislip found themselves swept into the lives of the monks as several manorial tenants had to provide horses and hospitality for them, carry letters and produce to distant manors and to prepare cheeses and other goods for dispatch to Bec.

5. The ditch and earthwork in 1975 when the ditch was waterlogged. Since the dry summers of the 1980s it has only been wet after periods of heavy rain.

THE PRIORY

During the Hundred Years War, Ruislip along with all the other possessions of French abbeys was classified as an Alien Priory and Extents (inventories) were taken on several occasions. The earliest shows that mainly wheat and oats had been grown in 1293 and a little barley, but peas and beans were stored in the granary from a previous year. Although there were a number of animals, the demesne was being managed for its produce which was the main source of income. The priory already had a chapel with ornaments

6 & 7. Two views of the late 13th century Great Barn. This is the only building at Manor Farm dating from the time of the Abbey of Bec's overlordship.

8. The Grange, Northwood. The Abbey of Bec's grange at Northwood was probably situated near this house.

worth £2 13s 4d and there was a watermill and a windmill. The watermill was probably along the Pinn near Clack Lane (an onomatopoeic word) and the windmill was almost certainly in Great Windmill Field on the modern Windmill Hill. Neither appears in any record later than the 15th century.

In 1324 the hall and rooms of the priory were in need of repair and there was a Guest House and three barns, one of which was said to lie northwards and southwards. This was almost certainly the Great Barn, which has been dated to the third quarter of the 13th century because of the style of its timber framing and joints. It is the oldest barn in Middlesex and second only to Harmondsworth Barn in size. It is of superior craftsmanship, built while the power of the priory was at its height and shortly before the long period of decline when Ruislip was an Alien Priory.

The hall, rooms and chapel may have stood on the motte, but were probably built on the flat ground of the bailey, in front of the present Manor Farmhouse. 'The old ruinated Friars' hall' was not pulled down until 1613.

The priory had two granges, one at Northwood where six ploughmen lived with a maidservant who made the pottage and another at Bourne, where a boy looked after oxen, presumably the plough animals. It probably stood in the field marked Priors' Field on Rocque's map.

The tenants of the manor appear in a customal dated c1245 and in court rolls, quarrelling with their neighbours over boundaries, trespassing in the lord's wood, letting their beasts into the lord's garden and committing adultery, for which Lucy Mill had all her tenements seized. The 150 property owning men and women named in the customal perhaps represent a population of some 750, roughly triple that of 1086.

Just under half had land in the open fields, varying in amount from about 10 to 100 acres, others had smaller crofts of land near their houses and all except seven freeholders, had to perform labour services for the lord, working on the demesne for three days eac! week. The Ruislip works seem to have been unusually onerous as even virgate (25 acres) holders and crofters were expected to work for three days a week. However, as early as 1245 it seems that Ruislip tenants could pay a higher rent to be quit of these tasks and only worked on the lord's demesne on special boondays.

Money was in short supply in Richard II's reign when royal exactions from Alien Priories were very heavy and Northwood was leased out to Roger Redinge and in 1384 to John St George and Joan his wife, to raise lump sums. In 1404 Henry IV granted all the Bec property in the Bailiwick of Ogbourne to the last Proctor-General, William de St Vaast, Thomas Langley, Dean of York, later Bishop of Durham and his son, John of Lancaster, later Duke of Bedford. William de St Vaast died very soon afterwards, ending Bec's long association with Ruislip.

Nowadays, Herlwyn Avenue recalls the abbey's founder and the Sacred Heart church has a social club called the Bec Club.

JOHN OF LANCASTER AND JOHN SOMERSET

By the time Prince John was created Duke of Bedford in 1414 he was in sole possession of Ruislip and the other Ogbourne properties and continued as lord of the manor until his death in 1436, when it was taken into the hands of the king, Henry VI. He granted it to his chancellor, John Somerset, the following year, with reversion to the University of Cambridge. After 1440 a commission was set up to settle the future ownership of Alien Priories and eight, including Ruislip, were finally granted to the College of Our Blessed Lady and St Nicholas at Cambridge (later known as King's College).

KING'S COLLEGE

King's College are still titular lords of the manor of Ruislip. As absentee landlords the Provost and Scholars chose to farm out the demesne, the woods and other manorial prerogatives, sometimes together and sometimes separately. The earliest lease in the King's College ledger books was to Thomas Betts in 1471. He leased both demesne and woods. Demesne leasing continued until 1872, when a decision was taken to retain the woods in hand and to let Manor Farm directly. Among interesting lessees were Roger More, Henry VIII's baker and the first Earl of Salisbury. From 1669 members of the Hawtrey family of Eastcote House and their descendants always held the demesne.

Many buildings were built or rebuilt during the College's ownership. The present Manor Farmhouse dates from about 1500 and the Little Barn, now used

9. The Manor Farm was built about 1500 to house the demesne farmer. The old priory which was described as 'ruinated' in 1613 probably stood in front of it.

10. The 18th-century cowshed with a dairy in front, now used as a Guide hut. The 19th-century stables on the right have a slate roof.

11. The Victorian granary standing on cast iron staddles, which was struck by lightning and burnt down in 1980.

12. The thatched 19th-century cow byre is on the left of this picture taken about 1937.

as the public library dates from the 16th century. The Guide Hut is an 18th-century barn and there are some Victorian stables. A 19th-century thatched cow byre and a granary on cast iron staddles have both been lost in fires in 1976 and 1980. A replacement Cow Byre opened in 1980 houses an exhibition room and cafe.

Manor Farm was called Ruislip Court until the 19th century and although a farmhouse it was also the manor house and the place where manor courts were held. The last was convened in 1925.

Two major surveys were undertaken for King's College in 1565 and 1750. The first covered the whole manor, listing the tenants and their cottages and land street by street and field by field, giving the abuttals, thus making possible the creation of a reasonably accurate map. In 1750 John Doharty of Worcester was commissioned to prepare a map of the demesne lands only. Apart from a 17th-century plan of Park Wood, the splendid Doharty map is the earliest extant of any part of Ruislip. The demesne of about 1900 acres included the Common Wood and Park Wood and formed a central band running from north to south down the manor.

These two surveys and court rolls and other documents preserved at King's College provide an increasingly clear picture of life in Ruislip during the last 500 years.

The College is remembered in King's College Road and King's College Playing Fields.

13. The pig sties alongside the Guide Hut, shown adjoining the Great Barn.

14. St Martin's 1795. The nave is lit by dormer windows and the vicar's vestry can just be seen sticking out from the chancel wall.

The Parish Church

St Martin's church stands at the centre of the old parish of Ruislip, close to Manor Farm. In its present form it dates from the mid-13th century, but the priest mentioned in the Domesday Book is likely to have had a church on the same spot. The walls are of flint rubble with dressings of Reigate and Tottenhoe stone at the corners and around the windows and the roof is covered with tiles and lead. A stone with chevron markings from the Norman period, found during recent work on the wall paintings, suggests that the earlier building was also stone built.

The founder of the church is unknown, but it could have been Wiward Wit as land owners often built churches on their estates and appointed priests in Saxon times. It is almost certain that Ernulf de Hesdin included the church in his gift of Ruislip to the Abbey of Bec; and Bishops of London from the time of Richard FitzNeal (1189-98) confirmed the appropriation to Bec until the late 13th century. William de Guineville who was appointed Proctor-General in 1242 is known to have been a vigorous administrator and is likely to have instigated the work of rebuilding the church. The population had greatly increased and as the congregation was swelled by the stewards and other Bec officials who had business at the priory, a beautiful new church was probably necessary and added to the prestige of the Abbey.

Ralph Truler (which means mason) mentioned in the customal of c1245, may have been working on the church. The nave has two arcades, that on the south being slightly earlier than the one on the north, but both appearing to have been built in the 1240s. Dormer windows along both sides of the nave were swept away during a major restoration by George Gilbert Scott in 1869-70.

The Duke of Bedford granted the spiritualities of all his churches, including Ruislip, to the Dean and Canons of Windsor in 1422 and they have been the patrons ever since. The church may have been in a poor state because of the prior's lack of funds during the long years when Ruislip was an Alien Priory, but if so there was no rush to restore it. The next reconstruction was not undertaken until the second half of the 15th century when the chancel and south aisle were rebuilt and a vestry was extended from the north wall of the chancel. The tower at the west end

15. St Martin's in modern times.

16. The nave about 1900, long before the Victorian reredos by Robert Lewis Roumieu was hidden behind a curtain.

was erected in stages during the century and the bell chamber was added c1500. At the same time the north aisle was rebuilt and the south aisle extended east to form a chapel.

By 1476 the Dean and Canons were farming the rectory, that is the right to collect the great tithes, and the responsibility for the rebuilding may have fallen on the lessee, John Walleston and the other members of the Walleston family who succeeded him.

Ralph Hawtrey married into the Walleston family and took over the rectory in 1532. His descendants continued to lease it until 1867, when all Windsor's ecclesiastical estates passed into the hands of the Ecclesiastical Commissioners.

CHURCH INTERIOR

Wall paintings covered the nave arcades in the 15th century. Recent renovation has made the Seven Deadly Sins on the north side much clearer; the corresponding Corporal works of Mercy on the south were overpainted with the figure of a man wearing apparel of c1530. There is also St Christopher in the south aisle and St Michael weighing souls above the door to the rood loft stairs.

The window glass is mainly Victorian, with some attractive scenes from the life of St Martin by Kempe in the chancel, installed as a memorial to the Reverend Thomas Marsh-Everett who died in 1900. Other memorials in the chancel are to the Hawtrey family and their descendants, the Deanes and their connections. A brass on the wall shows Ralph Hawtrey, from Chequers, who married Winnifred Walleston, a local heiress c1525. The monument to their grandson, Ralph who died in 1638 and his wife, Mary, has the most artistic merit, being sculpted by John and Matthias Christmas.

VICARS

The continuous list of vicars starts in 1327 with William de Berminton and contains only one local man, John Shorediche (1708-14), a younger son of the lord of the manor of Ickenham. Many of the vicars were minor canons of St George's, Windsor, as it was customary to offer livings within the Dean and Canons' gift to them in order of seniority. As they were required to have skill in music, St Martin's probably benefited from some musical vicars.

Religious changes of the 16th and 17th centuries seem to have had little effect upon Ruislip. Since George Whitehorne stayed in office right through the religious upheavals of the reigns of Henry VIII and Edward VI, it must be supposed that he and the people of Ruislip accepted the changes that were imposed upon them. He was deprived of the living during Mary's reign, but returned in 1559.

During the Civil Wars of the 17th century William Dring was ejected as 'a scandalous minister' – probably he failed to preach as many sermons as expected in those puritanical times - and was succeeded by Nathaniel Giles who sounds much more scandalous, for he was a proverb for litigiousness and used to preach with his pistol hung at his neck.

Only three vicars covered the 19th century at St Martin's. The value of the living had increased after the enclosure of the waste and commons in 1814 and by 1834 it was worth £462 per annum. The Reverend Daniel Carter Lewis died in that year and Windsor was flooded with applications. The letter of Christopher Packe, vicar of St Michael Bassishaw in the City of London is heartrending: 'That I should feel most anxious for a home in the country, you gentlemen, who are aware of the numerous losses I have sustained in my family during the eight years I have lived in my present residence in London cannot feel surprised. Five children have been snatched from me during that period and of the two remaining little ones the infant only of nine months has enjoyed health..... God knows how I long for the pure air of the country.'

17. The churchyard had many wooden graveboards, which ran lengthwise along the graves, but only four remain today. 'Cast us not away from thy presence, O Lord' is written on the one in the centre of the picture. The porch is in a bad way being supported by wooden buttresses. It was pulled down and replaced in 1896. The building on the right was the Old Bell public house until 1932. Vestry meetings sometimes adjourned there in the 18th century.

He came and stayed until his death 44 years later. He was a zealous clergyman, fighting the evils of drunkenness and gambling and riding up to Northwood for many years before a church was built there, to take divine service in a cottage set aside as a chapel. The hilly part of Bury Street which passes the Vicarage was known as Packe Hill.

Thomas Marsh-Everett who succeeded him (*Illustration* 19) established a tradition of musical concerts in the parish, at which he was a frequent performer and played a large part in civic affairs, being chairman of the first Ruislip Parish Council set up in 1895. The lych-gate in Eastcote Road commemorates him.

THE VICARAGE

The vicar of Ruislip had a house on the west side of Bury Street, north of the Pinn from before 1391 until 1981, somewhat distant from the church. It is uncertain how many buildings have stood on the site. Thomas Marsh-Everett married the daughter of L.J. Baker of Haydon Hall in 1882 and in preparation for his marriage had a handsome new vicarage built close to the old one which was demolished except for what was then a new wing and is now the Vicarage Cottage.

The new vicarage is built of a pleasant red brick, with gables, a tiled roof and interesting chimneys owing something perhaps to the architectural 'cottage style' employed by George & Peto on the Haydon Hall estate of Mr Marsh-Everett's father-in-law.

Later vicars found the house too large and it was sold to a private developer in 1981 and converted into flats in 1985. A house built in Eastcote Road in 1925, just opposite the church, has been the vicarage since 1983.

Earlier vicars had agricultural interests and lived off their glebe land, supplemented by the small tithes. Glebe was the land assigned to the incumbent of a parish as part of his benefice. Small tithes consisted of eggs, milk, pigs etc., and were harder to measure and collect than the great tithes of wheat etc., which

18. The fine monument by John and Matthias Christmas to Ralph Hawtrey who died in 1638 and his wife Mary, parents of Lady Bankes.

went to the rector. Before the enclosures Ruislip vicars had strips in the open fields and a 2½ acre croft near the vicarage, amounting to about 50 acres in all. Afterwards the glebe was increased to about 250 acres, partly to compensate for loss of tithes which were suppressed on the newly enclosed lands, and for the right to take firewood out of Park Wood.

Christopher Packe exchanged some outlying land with Sir Charles Mills (later Lord Hillingdon) for Little Manor Farm in 1877 and a farmhouse still called Glebe Farm was built on the former glebe in 1882. Thomas Marsh-Everett began selling the Northwood glebe for building development in the 1890s, though much of it is open space, being part of Haste Hill Golf Course, Northwood Recreation Ground and Allotment Gardens and Northwood Cemetery. Later vicars continued the process and only one field of the former glebe, near Clack Lane, remains today.

19. Revd. Thomas Marsh-Everett, Vicar of Ruislip (1878-1900)

20. The new wing of the old timber-framed vicarage was left standing in 1881 and is now the Vicarage Cottage.

21. The new vicarage built by Mr Marsh-Everett in 1881 in time for his marriage. The main entrance faced the River Pinn, but was moved to the Bury Street side of the house in 1938 by the Revd Derek Barnsley.

22. Little Manor Farm which Sir Charles Henry Mills (later Lord Hillingdon) exchanged with Christopher Packe in 1877, for glebe land in the southern part of the parish. It stands in the part of Howletts Lane which was renamed Arlington Drive.

23. Glebe Farm was built in 1882. Sir Charles Henry Mills' coat of arms can be seen on the gable. It stands in West End Road just behind the Polish War Memorial.

Park and Woodlands

Ruislip has extensive woodlands, more than 600 acres, in three woods called Park Wood, Copse Wood and Mad Bess Wood. They stretch across the northern upland part of the parish and are now managed as a recreational amenity by the local authority, but formerly they provided timber for building and the repair of houses, wood for fuel and fencing, and shooting. They are classified as ancient woodland and are remnants of the forest that once covered Middlesex. The oak is the predominant tree and provides the wood or timber while hornbeam forms the shrub layer or underwood.

PARK WOOD

Park Wood contains within it the boundary banks of the park for woodland beasts that was mentioned in the Domesday Book. Parks were used as game reserves and as larders for storing food on the hoof. Ruislip's park was an enclosure of about 300 acres within the vast tract of surrounding woodland. It was oval in shape and situated in the southern half of the present Park Wood and the area surrounded by Bury Street, Eastcote Road and Fore Street (meaning the front of the park). Massive earthbanks with an external ditch (30-35 feet total width) can still be traced through the middle of Park Wood from near the western entrance in Broadwood Avenue, curving round to the footpath near Grangewood School in Fore Street and as recently as the 1920s, before the widening of Bury Street and extensive building on the Manor Farm estate, the western and southern earthbanks could still be seen as well. There is a reference to stocking the park with 12 live does from the Archbishop of Canterbury's Harrow Wood in 1270 and to repairing the palings which must have topped the banks in 1436.

In later medieval times the southern portion of the park altered in character, land along the Pinn becoming meadows attached to the manor house and enclosed pasture. Perhaps to compensate the park was extended northwards to a stream (which now runs into the Lido) and enclosed with slightly less massive earthbanks, best viewed along the Fore Street edge of Park Wood.

24. The bank and ditch which once completely surrounded the Park for wild beasts mentioned in the Domesday Book.

THE COMMON WOOD (COPSE WOOD)

The rest of the woodland which stretched across what is now Poor's Field, Northwood and Haste Hill Golf Courses and Northwood Hills was known as the Great Common Wood. In the 16th century there were 860 acres used by the inhabitants of Ruislip for grazing animals and for collecting fuel: they were permitted to get what they could by hook or by crook (that is to pull down branches with a crook and cut off brushwood with a billhook) and to take the lop and top, but only the lord of the manor or his lessee could cut down the wood and underwood.

Robert Cecil, 1st Earl of Salisbury, who leased the demesne and woods at the beginning of the 17th century, drastically altered the Common Wood in 1608 by selling all the trees, wood and underwood, not at that time enclosed, thus clearing 568 acres and gaining £4000 for himself. Until the enclosures of 1814 that part of the Common Wood continued as common waste and the other 300 acres became Copse Wood.

MAD BESS WOOD

Here is an intriguing name, but alas, with no explanation of its origin, although many have been made up by fertile imaginations. The wood is what remains of Westwood Common in St Catherine's Manor. A survey made in 1586 shows that portions of woodland had been enclosed from the surrounding waste piecemeal over the previous few years. This accounts for the numerous earthbanks in the wood, surrounding the different pieces of woodland (*Ill.* 26).

In the 18th century the different areas were named North Riding, Mad Bess, Youngwood, Standell's Wood and Censor's Wood and it is only in recent years that Mad Bess has become the predominant name. Fifteen-year-old John Brill was battered to death in Youngwood in 1837, having been sent by John Churchill, the farmer for whom he worked, to mend fences. The murderers were almost certainly three local poachers who had a grudge against the boy for having given evidence against them some months previously. They were never brought to trial because when they were taken to view the body, it did not spurt blood in accordance with a widely held superstition that corpses would run with blood when their murderers were near.

MANAGEMENT*

The lords of the manor and the lessees derived a considerable income from the woods. In 1289 25% of the manorial income came from the sale of wood and underwood and from pannage (the tax paid by tenants for the right to graze their pigs on the acorns from Michaelmas to Martinmas).

The wood came from the oaks which were felled as required, always leaving at least 12 storiers to the

25. Old hornbeam coppice in Mad Bess Wood

26. Map of Mad Bess Wood showing the boundary banks dividing the various pieces of woodland which were enclosed piecemeal from Westwood Common during the Pagets' ownership.

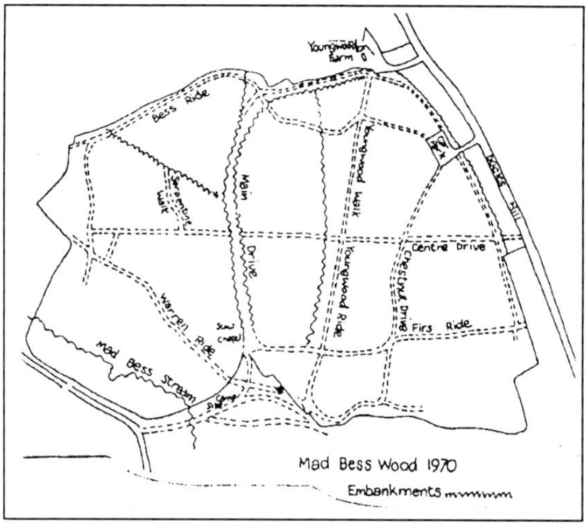

27. (Above) The Six Bells, built on newly enclosed land in Ducks Hill about 1810 by Samuel Salter the Rickmansworth brewer. It took the sign of a beer house which used to stand on the eastern corner of Breakspear Road and Howletts Lane. It was the scene of the inquest on John Brill's body in 1837 (see page 23) and of the wood sales.

28. (Top right) A scene in Park Wood. The oaks provided the wood or timber trees.

29. (Below) Coppicing in Mad Bess Wood in 1979, when it had been reintroduced as part of the new management plan.

30. The Woodmans, who were wood dealers, outside the barn at Woodman Farm, Bury Street at the turn of the century.

acre, following a statute of 1544 meant to preserve sufficient timber trees for shipbuilding. Management customs varied from time to time. In 1810 it was customary to leave 40 storiers to the acre: 20 could be felled after one year and the other 20 left for timber. During the Abbey of Bec's lordship, oaks from Ruislip Woods helped build several royal edifices, the Tower of London in 1339, Windsor Castle in 1344, Westminster Palace in 1346 and the Black Prince's manor of Kennington in the same year. Two royal purveyors, one of whom was a local man, requisitioned excessive amounts of timber in 1536, taking 300 oaks for paling the new park beside Westminster (St James's).

The underwood came from the hornbeam which was coppiced, that is cut down, leaving the stool which sprouted again sending up long, straight poles, suitable for pea and bean sticks and firewood. Areas were coppiced in rotation, the cycle varying from 7 to 15 years from century to century and wood to wood, depending upon climatic and growing conditions. By Victorian times, when gamekeepers preserved woodcock and pheasants for shooting parties, the cycle was not more than 12 years, that being the maximum height over which the pheasants could be driven.

Although most of the oaks were grown for timber, some were coppiced to increase the area of bark which was stripped from the cut poles and sold to local tanneries at Uxbridge and Rickmansworth. In one year in the 18th century 2477 yards of bark fetched £202 16s 6d, 14 loads of hoops £41 19s and the sale of the coppiced wood £436 15s 3d.

The woods provided seasonal employment for about 30 Ruislip men in the 18th century and helped whole families to eke out a living in the 1850s and 60s, when bundles of firewood were made up by women and children and sold on the London market by dealers. In 1851 eight men and boys living at Ruislip Common were woodcutters and 15 old men, women and boys were kindle makers.

From 1872 the woods were retained in hand by King's College and only sporting leases were let. Sedgewick's, the College agents, appointed a woodman to look after them. In March each year he marked the oaks which were ready for selling with white paint and a sale was held in a local public house, usually the Six Bells in Ducks Hill, but sometimes at the Black Horse in Eastcote Road. Wood dealers, having examined the timber beforehand, bid for stands of oak and felled those they bought in March or April.

The underwood was sold in October. The woodman marked the four to five acre lots by cutting the larger growth about 3 feet 6 inches or 4 feet above the ground

31. Woodsale Day at the Six Bells.

around the boundaries. The autumn sale seems to have been regarded as a general day out locally and drew a large attendance, not only of dealers, but of those looking for work and of lookers on. The coppice had to be cut, then sorted into sizes suitable for peasticks, beansticks, stakes and rods used exclusively for hedging. All the bundles were tied with withies (ties made from willow).

During the 1930s all three woods were acquired by the local authority and traditional management virtually ceased after the outbreak of the Second World War, so that the woods were becoming dark with a depleted flora, causing much local concern which came to a head in 1979. The Borough of Hillingdon set up a Woodlands Advisory Working Party composed of relevant council officials and representatives of local bodies and the Nature Conservancy. A long-term management plan was adopted, returning to a coppicing cycle (20 years) for the oak-hornbeam area and a thinning cycle elsewhere.

32. The Black Horse on Eastcote Road was an inn in the early 18th century and was probably altered after being struck by lightning in 1837. Woodsales were held there in Victorian times.

33. *Eastcote House with its 18th-century front and early 19th-century stucco; it was the home of the Hawtreys and their descendants from 1525.*

Families and their Houses

J. Norris Brewer writing in the *Beauties of England & Wales* in 1816, described Ruislip as 'a village of a rural character' whose farm buildings had 'an air of neatness and comfort' and where there were a few houses 'sufficiently capacious for the accommodation of retired gentility'. The houses he considered worthy of mention were Eastcote House, Haydon Hall and Highgrove. Although those great houses were perhaps the most imposing and the first two had been long established, there were already some other 'cottages' with 'pleasure grounds' where gentlemen, some retired from the services, others with businesses in London, could enjoy country life with reasonable access to town.

EASTCOTE HOUSE

Ralph Hawtrey (1494-1574), fourth son of Thomas Hawtrey of Chequers, came to Ruislip about 1525 and married Winnifred Walleston, a member of the family that leased the rectory. Winnifred's dowry was a cottage called Hopkyttes at Well Green, Eastcote. It became the Hawtrey's principal residence and was later known as Eastcote House. The Ruislip branch of the Hawtreys founded by Ralph and Winnifred re-

34. *The brass of Ralph Hawtrey and his wife Winnifred was once embedded in the floor of the south aisle of St Martin's. It is now on the south wall of the chancel.*

35. The roofspace of Eastcote House in 1964, shortly before demolition, showing some of the original timberwork.

tained the house until 1930 when Ralph Hawtrey Deane sold it and surrounding land to the Wembley (Comben & Wakeling) Land Company for building development.

Eastcote House within living memory was a stucco-fronted brick building, but this facade hid the original timber-frame which was revealed during demolition. Ralph Hawtrey or perhaps his son John Hawtrey (d 1593) is thought to have enlarged Hopkyttes and a later Ralph Hawtrey (1626-1725) may have covered it with a brick skin and made interior alterations towards the end of his long life. The 18th-century brick facade was given a fashionable stucco facelift about 1810, by Ralph Deane, a descendant.

THE HAWTREYS

The Hawtreys created a large estate in the parish by leasing the rectory from the Dean and Canons of Windsor (1532-1867), by leasing the demesne of the manor from King's College, Cambridge (1667-1872) and by acquiring land and farms in Eastcote. Their position as Justices of the Peace enabled them to supervise law and order in the area, influence the election of parish officers and view parish accounts. In the absence of a resident lord of the manor, the Hawtreys and their descendants the Rogers and Deanes, became the most influential gentry family and local squires. Most of the male Hawtreys who lived to maturity embraced the legal profession, becoming Barristers of Gray's Inn, Lincoln's Inn and Middle Temple.

LADY BANKES

However, it was a female Hawtrey, Mary the daughter of Ralph (1570-1638), who achieved national fame. She married Sir John Bankes, of Corfe Castle, Dorset, and twice defended it against the besieging Roundheads while her husband was away supporting Charles I. Unhappily she was betrayed by a servant and the castle was slighted. Thereafter the Bankes lived at Kingston Lacy. She is buried in St Martin's where her monument on the south wall of the chancel says that she had 'the honour to have borne with a constancy and courage above her sex a noble propor'con of the late calamities.' Lady Bankes Primary School in Ruislip Manor is named after her.

36. The Staircase at Eastcote House

37. The Cromwell Room at Eastcote House. The Hawtreys and Deanes were Justices of the Peace and this room is sometimes referred to as the Justice Room.

THE DEANES

The Ralph Hawtrey (d 1725) who lived to be 99, having outlived his sons and only grandson, left his estates to his grandaughter Jane Rogers. She died young and her 14-year-old daughter Elizabeth inherited all the estates in 1736. Elizabeth Rogers never married and became a redoubtable old lady defending her rights as lessee of the rectory, and strenuously opposing enclosure in any part of the parish. She also refused to answer the questionnaire devised by the Reverend Daniel Lysons when he was preparing his history of Middlesex parishes, as she considered his inquiries impertinent.

Ralph Deane (1782-1852), her cousin's grandson, was in possession by 1810 when her trustees had already instigated enclosure. The Ruislip Enclosure Award 1814 made the demesne and the rectory more valuable and Ralph Deane's estate more extensive – his personal estate was 462 acres, the rectory land 500 acres and the demesne 1900 acres (including the woods).

Ralph Deane was active in local affairs, usually heading subscription lists, as in 1840 when a new National School was built in Eastcote Road, and he attended Vestry Meetings. His son Francis was the last of the family to live at Eastcote House, the last to lease the rectory and the last to lease the demesne. He moved to East View, Uxbridge in 1878 and thereafter let the house to tenants and his son and grandson sold off the estate for building between 1920 and 1936.

SAMUEL MORTON PETO (1809-89)

The most interesting tenant of Eastcote House was Sir Samuel Morton Peto, building contractor and engineer, who lived there with his family from 1877 to 1886. He had been responsible for world-wide railway construction, had built the Lyceum in 1834, the St James's Theatre in 1835, the Reform Club 1836, Nelson's Column in 1843 and with his partner Grissell, the Houses of Parliament to Charles Barry's design in 1841. He was MP in turn for Norwich, Finsbury and Bristol, but alas became bankrupt in 1867. Eastcote was no doubt a rural retreat after a vigorous public life, and from here he instructed local agricultural labourers by assisting at Penny Readings, giving a talk on coal and its uses in 1877, and his family sang at local concerts.

38. *Sir Samuel Morton Peto, who lived at Eastcote House from 1877-86.*

39. *A dovecot was originally built by John Hawtrey before 1593 of which the bottom few rows of bricks remain. It was largely rebuilt in the 18th century. The potence or gallows which assisted in the collection of eggs and of young squabs remains inside.*

40. *Haydon Hall – Sir Thomas Franklin's hall of c1720 – can be seen flanked by Lawrence James Baker's additions.*

EASTCOTE HOUSE GARDENS

Public outcry against the proposed demolition of Eastcote House by Comben & Wakeling caused the Ruislip-Northwood Urban District Council to buy it along with 9.1 acres of the grounds in 1931. For nearly 30 years thereafter the house provided accommodation for Scouts, Guides, the Women's Institute, Welfare Clinics and other organisations, but was not properly maintained and having been declared unsafe for public use in 1962 was demolished in 1964. Today the former 17th-century coachhouse, the charming dovecot, first erected in 1601 and largely rebuilt in the 18th century, and the walled garden remain for public enjoyment.

HAYDON HALL

Quite close to Eastcote House stood another great house, Haydon Hall. It was built in 1630 by Lady Alice, Dowager Countess of Derby who was Lady of the Manor of Colham (which included Uxbridge) and who lived at Harefield Place, about four miles from Eastcote. Her reason for building this new house is unusual and stated in a letter: 'That if it should please God to call for me I might have a place to lay my stuff in out of my Lord Castlehaven's fingering'. She feared that Lord Castlehaven, a most vicious character, second husband of her eldest daughter, might seize any goods left at Harefield Place in the event of her death. In fact he was executed in 1631, having been tried by his peers, while Lady Alice lived on for another five years. Lady Castlehaven reverted to the name of her first husband, Lord Chandos after the disgrace and she, her son and grandaughters all owned Haydon Hall in succession down to 1675.

The new owner, George Sitwell, was an ironmaster from Eckington, Derbyshire and soon after moving to Eastcote married Elizabeth Hawtrey, the daughter of his near neighbour. Ralph Hawtrey lent him money on security of Haydon Hall in the 1690s when the ironworks failed and after he was declared bankrupt in 1693 his sister-in-law Mary's, second husband, Thomas Franklin bought it. He completely rebuilt the hall about 1720 and changed its name to Deanes.

When the Scropes of Cockerington owned it be-

41. The fine panelling in Haydon Hall shown in this photograph taken immediately before demolition in 1967, was not appreciated by Hillingdon Borough Council. A letter from the Town Clerk said that the hall contained 'nothing at all worthy of preservation'.

tween 1770 and 1789 they called it by the finer sounding Eastcote Park, but it reverted to Haydon Hall during the ownership of George Woodroffe 1799-1822. He was Chief Protonotary of the Court of Common Pleas, but also busied himself with local affairs. He sat on the local bench at Uxbridge, sometimes attended Vestry Meetings and was a member of a committee formed in 1812 to organise a Charity School.

METHODISM AT HAYDON HALL

Dr Adam Clarke a highly respected Methodist scholar and preacher lived at Haydon Hall from 1824-32. He established a place of worship in Redbournes, a cottage opposite the hall at the bottom of Joel Street in 1826 and elicited an immediate response from the poor people of Eastcote who filled it to overflowing and clamoured for a Sunday School where reading might be taught as well. By March 1827 a stable and coach house had been converted into a chapel and more than 70 children and some older people promised to attend the Sunday School. He died of cholera while staying in Bayswater in 1832, but his work continued at Haydon Hall until his daughter-in-law's second husband, John Harnett turned the Methodists out of the cottage. But the cause was strong in Eastcote and a new chapel was opened in 1848 in Field End Road.

42. Dr Adam Clarke, the Methodist Divine, who started Methodism in Eastcote, lived at Haydon Hall from 1824-32

43. Haydon Hall Lodge, designed in 1879 by George & Peto, cost £1100 and was built upon arches because of its proximity to the Pinn which was liable to flood.

WORK ON THE HAYDON HALL ESTATE

John Harnett lived at a cottage adjoining the estate and let the Hall to tenants. In 1864 the whole estate was purchased by Lawrence James Baker, a wealthy member of the London Stock Exchange, who transformed Sir Thomas Franklin's hall. He added two wings, greatly enhanced the pleasure grounds and built or rebuilt several cottages for estate workers, often employing Harold Ainsworth Peto, son of Sir Samuel Morton Peto of Eastcote House, and his partner Ernest George as architects. They designed the interior decorations of the Hall as well – rich chocolate brown paint and embossed maize-coloured paper in the principal drawing room, salmon colour in the library .

New Cottages on Eastcote High Road and the elaborate entrance lodge at the bottom of Southill Lane are some of the most attractive estate cottages, being half-timbered with incised plaster portraying flowers, foliage and faces. When Mr Baker's son, Lawrence Ingham Baker married Helen Agnes Peto, the architect's sister, the young couple went to live at Eastcote Lodge, a new house designed by the bride's brother and his partner on the site of a much older house which had been the residence of L.J. Baker's father.

SPORTING ESTATE

Mr Baker leased the shooting rights over Copse Wood, Park Wood and Manor Farm from King's College and he purchased the woodlands and much of St Catherine's Manor at a sale in 1873, so that he could shoot over 2000 acres – he actually owned 387 acres. He had two Keepers' Cottages built, one in Fore Street backing onto Park Wood and one at the bottom of Mad Bess Wood, complete with hatching pens. The annual bag was usually about 1000 pheasant and 30 woodcock.

44. New Cottages opposite Guts Pond (now a garden called Pretty Corner) on Eastcote Road is dated 1879 and belonged to Eastcote Lodge.

45. *The Gamekeeper's Cottage at the bottom of Mad Bess Wood. Another Keeper's Cottage in Coteford Close at the side of Park Wood and Homeside, Fore Street, built as a Cowman's cottage, are both of similar design.*

THE BENNETT-EDWARDS

Mr Baker moved to Ottershaw Park, Surrey in the mid-1880s, but kept up his local connections. A daughter married the vicar, Thomas Marsh-Everett, and he sat on the Ruislip Parish Council set up in 1894. The Hall was let to Captain Bennett-Edwards from 1886 and he and his wife, a novelist, stayed at Haydon Hall, opening its grounds for flower shows and Sunday School treats and providing and maintaining a cricket ground for the use of the Eastcote Cricket Club, which still plays there. Mrs Bennett-Edwards eventually bought the Hall and after her death in 1936, the house and 14.7 acres were purchased by Ruislip-Northwood Urban District Council in conjunction with the Middlesex County Council. Plans to turn it into a Civic Centre were frustrated by the outbreak of the Second World War and it suffered a similar fate to Eastcote House and was demolished in 1967. The grounds are open and some prefabricated buildings serve as public meeting rooms.

HIGHGROVE

Highgrove stands at Hale End, Eastcote. The Hale family is first mentioned in the customal of *c*1245 and early in the 18th century two female descendants, Martha Hale and Elizabeth Kelly shared the ownership of an old messuage and surrounding land. In 1747 the Reverend John Lidgould of Harmondsworth purchased one of the meadows and built Highgrove, a house with a central hall and flanking wings and a high tiled roof rising to a central peak above a balustrade at eaves level. Robert Turner, a maltster from Pinner lived there from 1758 and his son sold it to William Blencowe, a canon of Wells Cathedral in 1787.

46. *The Auction Catalogue for the 1834 sale following James Mitchell's death shows the only known picture of the earlier Highgrove.*

47. Highgrove, designed by Edward Prior for Sir Hugh Hume-Campbell and built in 1881.

48. Sir Hugh Hume-Campbell.

49. Eleanor Warrender as a nurse during the South African War.

The house appears to have been let from the beginning of the 19th century to John Humphrey Babb, who eventually bought it from another member of the Blencowe family in 1813. He was Deliverer of the Vote in the House of Commons and it was his successor in that post, James Mitchell, who was the executor of his will and who moved to Highgrove in 1825. After his death in 1833 Mrs Mitchell offered it for auction.

THE WARRENDERS AND HIGHGROVE

Lt General Joseph Fuller bought Highgrove in 1834. His only child, Juliana, married Sir Hugh Hume-Campbell of Marchmont in October 1841 only a few days before her father's death. After a disastrous fire on 16th November 1879 destroyed the house, they employed Edward Prior, a pupil of Norman Shaw, to design the present building. Lady Hume-Campbell had no children and the house was inherited in 1894 by the Warrenders, her husband's grandchildren through the daughter of his first marriage.

Eleanor Warrender and her brother Hugh made their permanent home in Eastcote after the First World War. Both were friendly with Jenny Churchill, Hugh apparently being in love with her, which may account for Winston Churchill having spent part of his honeymoon at Highgrove. The house was sometimes let to the Dowager Queen of Sweden, who retired there for her health for short periods.

Eleanor Warrender was a great benefactress to the neighbourhood - she provided an Institute for men opposite St Martin's in 1907 and Church Rooms in Bury Street in 1911. While working with the French Red Cross during the war she was received into the Roman Catholic church and in 1921 founded the Sacred Heart church in Ruislip High Street; she also started the Eastcote and Pinner Girl Guides and was District Commissioner for many years. She sold 10½ acres of her grounds to the council in 1935 for a children's playground, now Warrender Park and at the same time another 13 acres to Ideal Homes for building development.

Miss Warrender offered Highgrove to service personnel during the Second World War and it was used by English and American officers from Northolt Aerodrome. After her death in 1949, Ruislip-Northwood Urban District Council bought it and later made it over to the Middlesex County Council to be converted into an old people's home and half-way house. Despite another bad fire in 1978 it has been carefully restored by the Borough of Hillingdon and provides temporary accommodation for homeless families.

NORTHWOOD GRANGE AND THE ABBEY OF BEC'S GRANGE AT NORTHWOOD

A house, dating in part from the 15th century, stands in Rickmansworth Road, Northwood, called The Grange. The eastern end, probably of 16th century date, was a separate cottage until joined on in the 1860s and the western end was built on as a library about 1890. The eastern end is now a separate house, Green Close. The Grange is believed to stand either on or near the site of the Abbey of Bec's grange at Northwood. Another old house stood close by until the land was redeveloped in 1932 and both houses were in the ownership of Roger Arnold, a large landowner in 1565. John Rowe, Secretary of the New River Company, purchased them both in 1809. He possibly lived at the old house and let what is now the Grange as a farm. He was interested in horticulture and planted many interesting trees in the grounds, some of which are still there. He bought several farmhouses over the next few years, building up a large estate, most of which was sold by his son, John Paul Rowe, also of the New River Company, to Nathaniel Soames of Gravely, Stevenage in 1832.

50. The Grange, Northwood. This is a complicated building with a 15th-century block at the west end (the left of the picture) and a range built about 1600 to the east. Dr Nash built a library and added several ecclesiastical antiquities in the 1890s. The cottage/chapel just seen on the extreme right of the picture is now a separate house called Green Close.

NATHANIEL SOAMES

Mr Soames added to the estate, making it the largest in Northwood. He and his wife, Rebecca, lived at the old house and took a special interest in church affairs. He was a churchwarden at St Martin's and, worried about the number of Northwood cottagers who were not taking the four mile walk to church each Sunday, he fitted up the cottage that is now Green Close as a chapel, where the Reverend Christopher Packe or a curate read divine service. It reverted to its former use after the opening of Holy Trinity in 1854.

PART OF THE EASTBURY ESTATE

In 1864 Soames sold the entire estate of 279 acres to David Carnegie of Eastbury, a house just over the county boundary into Hertfordshire. Mr Carnegie appears to have set about refurbishing the Grange as soon as he became its owner and the farmhouse and cottage/chapel were joined together to become the principal residence and the old house seems to have become servants' quarters and perhaps stables. It was let to Robert Dunlop 'late of Her Majesty's Bengal Service', then to George Cheetham, son of a cotton mill owner from Stalybridge, Cheshire.

LAST PRIVATE OWNERS

When Mr Carnegie sold the entire Eastbury estate in 1887, the Grange was sold to Dr Llewellyn Nash, a Welsh medical practitioner from Hong Kong, who took a great interest in Egyptian archaeology. He built the library and added several antiquities to the Grange, one being a medieval screen from a London church. He probably gathered up the large pieces of flint and constructed the arch and niche which give the grounds a faintly ecclesiastical air. His daughters spoke in their letters of hearing the soft tread of monkish footsteps after dark!

The last private owner of the Grange was Colonel Blaythwaite who died in 1929. By 1932 the house and grounds were in the possession of the builder W.A. Telling and due for redevelopment but at this point Mrs Garrett, founder of St Helen's School, stepped in and generously bought the house (excluding Green Close at the eastern end). She was a devout churchwoman and converted the ground floor into a meeting place for parochial organisations and upstairs into two flats. It was requisitioned during the war and made over to the Ruislip-Northwood Urban District Council afterwards. It now belongs to the Borough of Hillingdon and is used for public purposes.

51. Northwood Hall was built onto the older Maze Farm in 1851 by Daniel Norton and has two overmantels from the Crystal Palace Exhibition. It is now Denville Hall, a rest home for retired members of the acting profession.

52. Arthur Nichols of Park Farm Dairy on his milk round in Northwood. Park Farm was the Home Farm of Northwood Hall.

NORTHWOOD HALL (DENVILLE HALL)

Denville Hall in Ducks Hill, Northwood, a gothic style mansion, took on its present form about 1851, when Daniel Norton (1806-88) a timber merchant associated with the Uxbridge milling family, rebuilt an old house called Maze Farm. Thereafter it was known as Northwood Hall and Northwood Park. In 1861 this was the largest household in the parish. He and his wife, Louisa, had six sons and three daughters and were looked after by five female servants.

Mr Norton formed the 196-acre estate by buying up neighbouring properties, demolishing the buildings and throwing the land into his park. He also acquired Park Farm, which became the Home Farm. He built a pretty cottage orné for his lodge and attractive stables and a coach house. The pleasure grounds were complete with a lake and two battlemented towers for summer houses, only one of which remains.

53. Mary Puddifont, lodgekeeper, was living with her husband James, who was a gardener, in this newly-built cottage orné in 1851.

54. Mr Parish and Mary Woodman sitting outside Park Farm c1910.

He and his family were prominent members of the newly formed parish of Northwood. His son, another Daniel Norton became chairman of the first Ruislip Parish Council in 1894 and was active in local affairs. The estate was sold in 1902 and Mount Vernon Hospital was built on the northern part. The house became a boys' school for a time, then stood empty until being bought by Alfred Denville MP in 1925 and converted into a rest home for retired members of the acting profession.

RUISLIP PARK

Park House, one of the most easily overlooked historic houses on Ruislip High Street, stands end on to the street and modern appendages: a florists', a children's clothing shop and an estate agent's office, prevent passers-by from viewing it properly and seeing that an old house lurks in the background. The small, gentleman's estate of 40 acres bounded by the High Street, the Oaks, Sharps Lane and Ickenham Road was created by Harry Edgell, Esq, who acquired the land piecemeal between 1790 and 1827 and 'improved' an old house. He was a barrister-at-law and related by marriage to Ralph Deane of Eastcote House, their wives being sisters. He sold the estate in 1832 to Orlando Stone, a City linen-draper who remained until 1840.

Many other short-term owners followed who let it out occasionally. George Barton Kent, grandson of the founder of the Brush Manufacturing Company, died there suddenly in July 1890, having only been resident for about seven months. Nevertheless, he was held in great esteem locally and a hundred of his London employees joined the mourners at his funeral at St Martin's.

In 1906 the estate was divided into building plots and sold very slowly at a series of auctions and through private transactions over the next twenty years.

The house was taken by F. Brewer Esq., who was in the tobacco business and was a friend of Edward VII. He and his sister lived there in some state, with a butler and staff until the late 1920s, when they moved to Thame. The house was rented by the Royal British Legion Club from 1930-46, who then purchased it. The Ruislip Branch of the British Legion now occupy the premises.

THE HOUSE

The house has a white stucco front, a balustrade round the eaves, sash windows and a pretty iron veranda. The auction catalogue of 1906 describes the accommodation as 12 bedrooms, a spacious square entrance hall, dining room, elegant drawing room, comfortable library and that prerequisite of a gentleman's house, a billiard room. This imposing mansion stood in equally attractive grounds with two sheets of ornamental water, a rookery, shrubbery, walled kitchen garden, greenhouse and vinery. Today the whole estate is built over and police houses in The Oaks stand exactly on the site of one of the ponds.

55. Park House, Ruislip.

56. Park Lodge at the corner of Ickenham Road and the High Street in 1931.

57. The Church House has been called the Almshouses since the mid-19th century. This photograph, taken about 1905, shows from the right a pair of cottages belonging to Manor Farm (demolished in 1976), the lodge to Manor Farm (now a public convenience), the Post Office and the outbuildings of the George, where Mr Hailey had a greengrocer's business. Beyond the Almshouses can be seen the end of a cottage joined to the Old Bell. It was taken down for road widening in 1927.

Caring for the Poor

The Elizabethan Poor Law of 1601 placed the burden of poor relief upon the parish, which it obliged to provide asylum and relief for the aged and infirm, give work to the able-bodied poor and apprentice poor children to a trade. The scheme was to be financed by a rate levied on property and administered by officials known as overseers of the poor, working within the framework of the vestry.

THE CHURCH HOUSE

The earliest evidence of the new poor law at work in Ruislip was the provision of accommodation for the impotent poor in 1616-17. A house built on the corner of Eastcote Road, backing onto the churchyard about 1570 and owned by the Harker family, was turned into ten small back-to-back cottages, each with one room upstairs and one room downstairs. Overseers of the poors' accounts abound in references to payments in money or kind, to poor people lodged at the 'Church House'.

June 1665	Widow Fearne of the Church House several times in her sickness 13s 0d
Mar 1666	Paid to John Bates for carrying 50 bavins (bundles of kindling) to Widow Fearne 1s 9d
1726	Moving three women to the Church House, my cart horse 15s 0d Paid the carpenter taking down the beds and setting them up 3s 0d

Although the Church House most frequently sheltered widows, a number of births occurred there and there are a few references to families and casual poor in residence. In 1679 a beggarman's wife was brought to bed there and in 1787 the vestry agreed to give poor families in the Church House 'a bed and bolster, a pair of blankets, a pair of sheets and a rugg each.' The 19th-century census returns show mainly widows, but one family, the Bowdens were there in 1861 with seven children and the mother (by then widowed) was still there with one daughter and a son in 1891.

Four of the little cottages were knocked together and modernised for the use of Mr Casemore, the verger in 1938. One of the cottages was given to the Guides in 1950 and when the last elderly resident died in 1954 her cottage became a Rover Den. The middle four cottages were slightly modernised and

58. Mr Casemore, verger at St Martin's.

were used by curates until 1975. By then the building was very dilapidated and threats of demolition were not finally averted until 1980, when restoration work began. There are now four flats and one maisonette held by the Harding Housing Association on a 75-year lease.

THE WORKHOUSE

Ruislip Vestry built a workhouse in 1789 on waste-land south of Copse Wood. Its first governor, John Burbidge, contracted to care for the poor in the house for £353 5s per annum, making what profit he could from the baking and laundry done by the paupers and from the sale of garden produce. The contract made with Martin Webber in 1830 laid down that the weekly diet was to include at least four hot dinners with good butcher's meat and plenty of fresh vegetables and good small beer every day. Children were to receive lessons in reading and spelling.

An inventory taken in 1795 (see page 45) when the first governor died lists 22 inmates, five men, four lads, 12 women and one girl. The accommodation included a bedlam, where vagrant lunatics who wandered into the parish could be confined. The numbers of paupers varied with agricultural conditions. In

59. Ruislip Workhouse was built in 1789. It is an almost exact replica of Harefield Workhouse 1782.

60. Jeremiah Bright's Bread Cupboard 1697, when it hung in the tower. Nowadays it is to be found in the north aisle. *(See page 45)*

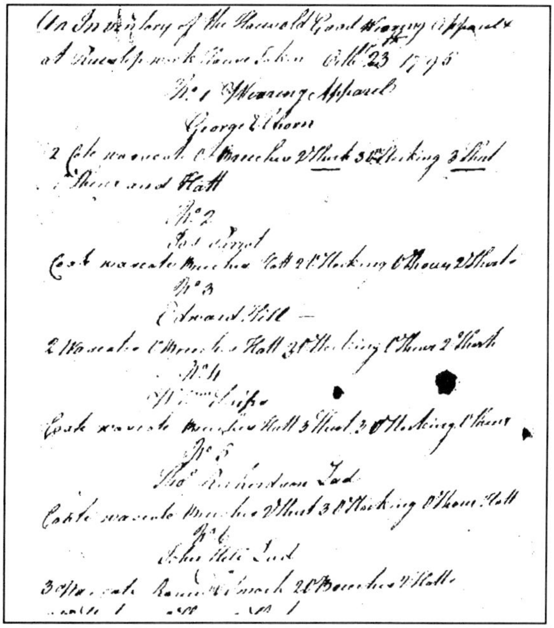

61. This page from the 1795 inventory describes the wearing apparel of the inmates.

62. Lady Juliana Hume-Campbell of Highgrove, who provided coal for the poor of Eastcote.

1830, a particularly depressed year, there were 40, but about 20 seems to have been the usual number.

Ruislip became part of the Uxbridge Union after the 1834 Poor Law Ammendment Act. From August 1836 indoor paupers from Harefield, Ickenham and Northolt were lodged at Ruislip, so that the other parish workhouses could be sold to raise money for a new Union House. This was opened at Hillingdon in August 1838 and Ruislip Workhouse was sold to Ralph Deane of Eastcote House, who converted it into six tenements. In 1921 his grandson, Ralph Hawtrey Deane, sold it to a Northwood builder, William Page, but shortly afterwards an architect, Waldo Emerson Guy, bought it, restored it and added a wing, and this old workhouse still stands as a private house in beautiful grounds.

PARISH CHARITIES

Private charity continued alongside the parish relief dispensed by the overseers of the poor out of the poor rate. Most of the endowed charities stipulated that the recipients should not be getting money from the parish as well.

In April 1717 Richard Cogges made over two closes of meadow in Fore Street called Perrycrofts, backing onto Park Wood, to the churchwardens of Ruislip who were to let them and distribute the money to needy people. Two thirds of the money was to go to Eastcote residents and one third to Westcote residents. The land is now let to a riding stables.

Jeremiah Bright, son of a former vicar of Ruislip, placed a handsome Bread Cupboard in the church in 1697 and presumably gave the churchwardens money for the bread. In 1721 he transferred responsibility to the Leathersellers' Company, of which he was master, giving them £150 covenanted so that the Company would pay £6 per annum to the Ruislip churchwardens and overseers, to provide 12 twopenny loaves every Sunday and 12 sixpenny loaves every Christmas Day. The 10 shillings left over was given to the vicar for his trouble in supervising the charity and helping to choose the recipients. Bread continued to be placed on the shelves until 1955. In 1915 the trustees decided that if people did not attend church to receive the loaves, bread left would be given to the occupants of the Church Houses on Monday morning!

Elizabeth Rogers (died 1803) directed her executors to place £380 in the 3% Consols and from the proceeds the churchwardens were to pay two guineas to the vicar on the first Sunday after Easter, provided that he had preached a sermon on Good Friday morning. The residue was to be distributed among such poor families as most regularly attended divine service.

Two charities were specifically for Eastcote families. Henrietta Howard provided for beef and bread to be given to 25 families on Christmas Eve and

63. Northwood Cottage Hospital, Pinner Road, was built as a War Memorial after the First World War and started in the VAD Hospital's premises in Hallowell Road. This new building was opened in 1925. It received donations from the Ruislip Cottagers' Allotments' Charity.

blankets to six families every New Year's Day. In 1918 the vicar found that he could not obtain blankets for five shillings and started giving money instead. Lady Juliana Hume-Campbell who died in 1886 left £10 per annum for coal.

All the above charities were consolidated as the Ruislip Non-ecclesiastical Charities in 1897 and amalgamated with the Ruislip Cottagers' Allotments' Charity in 1993.

RUISLIP COTTAGERS' ALLOTMENTS' CHARITY

Great Poor's Field between Park and Copse Woods, Little Poor's Field behind the Six Bells and the Eastcote Allotment on the east side of Joel Street were set aside for cottagers to graze their animals at the time of the enclosures. Few cottagers had animals and many sold their grazing rights for a few shillings.

After 1882 income was gained by renting pasturage and sporting rights over the Poor's Fields and the Eastcote Allotment was leased to the Ruislip-Northwood Small Holding and Allotment Society from 1909 and is still used as allotment gardens.

From the income of this charity, donations were made to various local Institutes to provide books and newspapers and to the Cottage hospitals which treated local people. Once or twice assistance was given with the costs of emigration, the purchase of tools for a boy starting an apprenticeship, and an outfit for a girl going into service; but mostly coal or coal and grocery vouchers were provided. The money is now invested and gifts are made to Old People's Homes at Christmas time.

Great Poor's Field was conveyed to Ruislip-Northwood Urban District Council in 1939 and is now public open space. Little Poor's Field was sold to the Ruislip-Northwood & Uxbridge Crematorium Joint Committee in 1961 and now forms the south-eastern portion of the crematorium grounds.

Farming the Land

BEFORE THE ENCLOSURES

Agricultural practice changed little in Ruislip from medieval times until the enclosure of the common fields and waste between 1804 and 1814. Individual farm houses had lands scattered throughout the common fields of Westcote or Eastcote. An undated, but late 18th-century map of King's End Farm, shows the farmhouse with its barn, cartshed and other outbuildings, surrounded by an orchard and enclosed meadows and pasture, but with its arable strips between quarter of a mile and two miles distant. In the mid-16th century 40 houses (farms) had common field land attached to them, but the number had declined slightly to 35 by the beginning of the 19th century.

The prosperity of the parish depended upon agriculture. The 1801 census showed that 493 out of a total 1014 inhabitants were employed on the land. Most were agricultural labourers working on the farms. The farmers were all tenants, leasing the farms annually from large landowners, like Mrs Rogers of Eastcote House, who owned Cuckoo Hill Farm, St Catherine's Farm, Fore Street Farm, Park Farm and Sigers. She at least was a resident landowner. Priors Farm belonged

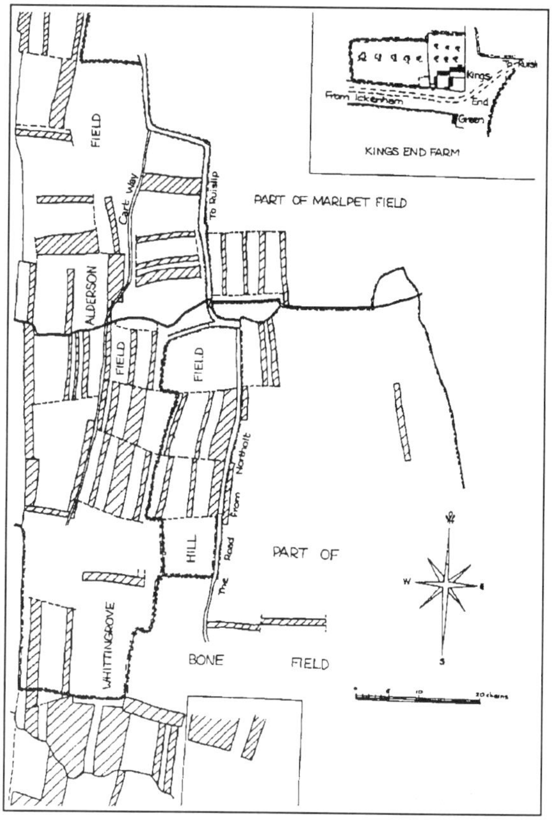

65. *A late 18th-century map of King's End Farm showing its land scattered throughout the common fields.*

64. *Cuckoo Hill Farm in 1978. Nowadays with modern windows the building belies its age.*

66. Sigers was once part of the Eastcote House estate. From 1910 it was the home of Sir Kenneth Goschen, Governor of the Bank of England, who held fêtes in the grounds to raise money to build St Lawrence's church.

67. Primrose Hill Farm, which the Hilliards eventually sold to Edwin Shatford Ewer sometime before 1910. Members of the Weedon family were tenant farmers there from before 1850 to the end of the century.

68. The Old Shooting Box was originally three small cottages and there were three others in front on the roadside, one being Eastcote Post Office in the 1860s and 70s.

69. *Southcote Farm stood on Ladygate Lane on the site of Whiteheath Junior School.*

70. *St Catherine's Farm, Catlin's Lane, Eastcote.*

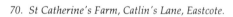

to Robert Child of Osterley Park and all the farms in St Catherine's Manor were the property of William Shepherd of Frome, Somerset and his sister-in-law, Miss Lewin. There were 108 proprietors, but only 49 of them lived in the parish and two thirds of the landowners with more than 50 acres were absentees.

Several of the tenant farmers owned property as well. John Bray rented Primrose Hill Farm from Edward Hilliard, but owned three cottages on Eastcote High Road, which used to stand in front of the Old Shooting Box. The labourers lived in this type of small cottage, paying a small rent.

John Middleton, who wrote a report on Middlesex for the Board of Agriculture in 1798, was particularly scathing about the practice of fallow, an idea which he believed to be 'now exploded in every part of the County, except in Ruislip and Ascot (Eastcote)...' He recommended that after enclosure the new fields should be turned over to hay in most parts of the county, as he thought that the proximity of the London market would double profits within 21 years.

Mrs Rogers' death in 1803 precipitated Ruislip Enclosure. The trustees of her will carried most of the other proprietors with them and a Bill was obtained in 1804 and the final award in 1814. The map is dated 1806.

72. Old Pond Farm, erected by Ralph Deane as an agricultural labourer's cottage, was called New Pond Farm until King's College put up a new farmhouse (now Ruislip Nursing Home) of that name nearby in 1872.

73. Haystacks at Manor Farm in the 1920s. Richard Ewer used to win prizes for his ricks.

71. The barn at Mill House being demolished in March 1936. It had housed the works of Gurney & Ewer from before the First World War. EMI is now on the site.

74. Northwood Farm, built about 1827 on newly-enclosed waste allotted to King's College, has a slightly earlier barn alongside.

NEW FARMHOUSES

Several new farmhouses were built on the newly enclosed land. A barn was built on former waste allocated to King's College in 1816 and Northwood Farm, in which Ralph Deane lodged his bailiff, was erected beside it about 1827. The College leased it to T. Ferguson Esq. for golf links in 1902 and it was subsequently purchased by Northwood Golf Club.

Ralph Deane built Bourne Farm in South Ruislip before 1820 and New Farm in Northwood *c*1880, to make the farming of the new rectory allotments easier., and he also erected Old Pond Farm in West End Road and a new Priors Farm about 1835. King's College built New Pond Farm nearby.

HAY

The predicted changeover to hay production came fairly slowly over a period of about 20 years. According to the Reverend John Roumieu, curate to Christopher Packe, the change was not beneficial to the labourers, as a large work force was only required at haymaking time, and he noted that poor families turned to kindlewood manufacture to make up their income.

Although their numbers went down, agricultural workers continued to be the largest occupational group in Ruislip throughout the 19th century. In 1861 there were 39 farmers, four farm bailiffs, 15 farmers' sons, 12 farm carters, six haybinders, one farm servant, two shepherds and 248 agricultural labourers, making up 60% of the workforce. The haybinders looked after the hay in the stacks. Those at Manor Farm were always famous for their neatness and often won competitions. The hay was taken regularly to the London markets at Fulham and Mark Lane and the horses were so familiar with the routes that stories abound of carters asleep on the wagons, for they left Ruislip in the early hours of the morning, leaving their horses to do the navigation.

75. Mill House, Bury Street, associated with the Ewer family for 350 years.

76. *Henry James Ewer (1849-1916) outside Manor Farm.*

THE EWERS

The most prominent farming family in 19th-century and early 20th-century Ruislip was the Ewers. They had been in the parish since the late 16th century when Richard Ewer bought Mill House in Bury Street. James Ewer (1773-1857) lived at Hill Farm from 1814 until his death. This he leased from the Clarkes of Swakeleys while he let out Mill House. Two of his sons, James and Richard, succeeded him at Hill Farm and his grandson, another James, finally purchased it at the Swakeleys' Auction in 1922. Another of his sons, Edwin, lived at Wilkins Farm on the High Street, which was owned by the Hilliard family and Edwin's son, Edwin Shatford Ewer, lived at the newly-built Primrose Hill Farm from the time of his marriage in 1910. Edwin Shatford bought both farms from the Hilliards in 1912.

Henry James Ewer (1849-1916), grandson of the first James's brother Henry, was born at Crows Nest Farm in Breakspear Road, just in the parish of Harefield. He farmed at Dormer's Wells in Southall and at Southcote Farm in Ladygate Lane, before moving to Manor Farm in 1886, where he stayed until his death. His son, Richard, stayed at Manor Farm until most of the farmland had been sold off by King's College for building development and Manor Farm itself had been given to Ruislip-Northwood Urban District Council for the people of Ruislip.

Edwin and Henry James Ewer were both on the first Ruislip Parish Council established in 1895 and Henry James was elected to the Ruislip-Northwood Urban District Council when it was set up in 1904.

77. *This picture, taken at a ploughing match held in Ruislip in 1934, was used as an advert for Gurney & Ewer. The firm specialised in farm machinery.*

78. (Above) Sherley's Farm – now The Barn Hotel – with members of the Collins family outside.

79. (Left) The new Field End House Farm built by William Lawrence in 1850.

80. *A ploughing match at Ruislip, 1934.*

81. Cannons Bridge Farm, Bury Street in 1942. Cottages were recorded at Cannons Bridge in 1434, but this building dates from the 16th century. The Wilshin family let it to the Brills, Lavenders and Tobutts during the Victorian period. They were connected with farming, being hay dealers, wood dealers and hay binders. By the 1950s the house was in a bad state, and had an addition tacked on to the front. Mr and Mrs Brown restored and extended it in 1958.

82. Haydon Hall Farm in 1946. It stood in Joel Street near the junction with Wiltshire Lane, where Ascott Court now stands.

83. Woodbine Cottage was built in three stages between the 16th and 18th centuries. It was described as a cottage and tile house in 1769. By 1845 Francis Woodman, a haydealer, was in occupation.

The Local Mines

BRICK AND TILE MAKING

The basement beds of the London Clay and Reading Beds, around the edges of the Common Wood have a plastic clay suitable for making tiles and there are references to tile kilns in Northwood from the late 14th century. Three tile houses are mentioned in 1565, one being on the site of Park Farm, one close by and the other at Kiln Farm. Tilemaking was also associated with the southern area of St Catherine's Manor called Tile Kilns (now Tile Kiln Lane) from 1448 until the beginning of Victoria's reign. Three messuages had tile houses in 1587, Clack Farm and Woodbine Cottage probably being two of them. All the tilemakers had to pay 1000 tiles a year to the lords of their respective manors in addition to their rent.

Bricks were made by Thomas Wetherlye at his 'brick place', Eastcote, probably Park Farm, in 1565 and there are references to brickmakers in the 17th and 18th centuries. Small, temporary brickfields, where the bricks were fired in clamps, were sometimes opened to produce enough bricks for a particular building. It is said that the pond in the grounds of Denville Hall is where the clay for the bricks was dug. A brickfield in West End Road open for only six months in 1866 seems to have made the bricks for the Bedingfield Place cottages. However there was some brickmaking on a commercial scale in both Northwood and Eastcote in Victorian and Edwardian times.

The Kirby family of Northwood made bricks at Kiln Farm until the 1850s, but there was only one brickmaker recorded in the 1861 census and none in 1871. However the land around Sandpit Hill Cottage in Hills Lane became a brickfield owned by the

84. The railway bridge in Rickmansworth Road built with bricks from Elkington's brickfield. It was replaced by the iron bridge in August 1961.

85. Park Farm in Field End Road seems to have been Thomas Wetherlye's 'brick place' in 1565. In the 19th century it was the home farm of the Eastcote House estate.

86. Kiln Farm is a timber-framed house dating from the 16th century, when it was William Winchester's 'tile place', but its age is hidden by the rendering. A wing was added in 1893. The gentleman in the doorway is Sir Christopher Cowan (1890-1979), who was Chairman of Middlesex County Council in 1956 and High Sheriff of Middlesex in 1960.

87. The chalk mine on the corner of Dene Road and Green Lane. Layers of flint can be seen in the walls.

Northwood Brick Company and was later known as Elkington's brickfield. William Prince was the foreman in 1881 and his son, William was working under him as a brickfield labourer. The bricks for the railway bridge built across Rickmansworth Road in 1886, were made there and the young William lived long enough to see the bricks he had made broken up, when the iron bridge replaced it in August 1961. The brickfield was run by Thomas Elkington at the turn of the century. He made London stock bricks. The brickfield had closed down before 1914. The houses of Highfield Crescent were built around the eastern edge of the brickfield in 1929.

Thomas Elkington ran another brickfield in Cheyney Street, Eastcote from 1896 to 1904, where red facing-bricks, moulded bricks and tiles were manufactured – some of these may be seen in houses between Marsh Road and Cannon Lane in Pinner.

SAND AND CHALK

Sand and chalk mining was closely associated with brickmaking and several shafts have been found in Northwood, causing great consternation when they suddenly open up in gardens. A chalk mine at the corner of Green Lane and Dene Road (chalk mines are sometimes called dene holes) is 67 feet deep and has three galleries ending in apsidal ends. The miners were members of the Kirby family who worked in the mines from 1822 to 1832 on a seasonal basis, starting each spring. As may be seen in *Illustration* 89, they scratched their names, initials and the dates in the surface of the chalk. Chalk was sometimes used in brickmaking, and some was made into lime.

Sand was also mined. A sand mine owned by Ralph Deane is mentioned in rate books around 1837-8, on the land that was later Elkington's brickfield. In December 1992 a deep cylindrical hole opened up in a garden in Highfield Crescent and turned out to be a shaft lined with red facing-bricks. It is almost certainly a sandmine shaft sunk through the London Clay to the Reading Beds, to get at the white Reading Sands. 19th-century geologists refer to white sand being dug out of open pits on the lower part of the nearby common and there are memories of Thomas Elkington obtaining sand through an underground tunnel. Two sandminers are recorded in the 1851 census, one being Edward Kirby, living at Kiln Farm and four in 1861.

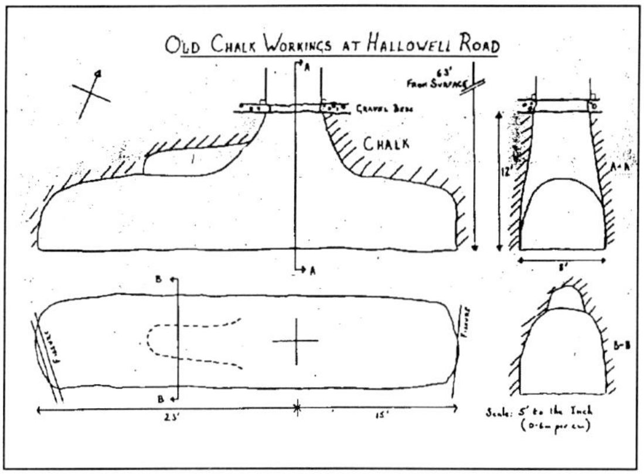

88. Cross section and plan of a chalk mine in the garden of a house in Hallowell Road, Northwood. It was explored in May 1978. The mine had probably been abandoned after a short time because of flooding through the two fissures.

89. Kirby family graffiti in Green Lane chalk mine.

Trains into Ruislip

THE EASTBURY ESTATE

Eastbury lies in Hertfordshire, just over the county boundary, and was originally in the parish of Watford. In 1854 Lord Ebury of Moor Park generously endowed a church for Northwood, Holy Trinity, and a new Northwood parish was created including Batchworth Heath and Eastbury. David Carnegie of Stranraer, Lochernhead, Perthshire purchased the estate in 1857. His family was connected with the Earls of Southesk whose coat of arms is a spread eagle, an emblem used to embellish the new mansion which he built in Scottish baronial style soon after becoming owner. This house later became a girls' school, then a somewhat dubious country club called the Chateau de Madrid and it was taken over by the RAF during the Second World War, becoming the headquarters of Coastal Command afterwards. Although fire destroyed most of the house, one room seems to have survived as part of the Officers' Mess.

David Carnegie increased the estate by buying all the farms of the Grange estate – Greenhill Farm, Green Lane Farm, Kiln Farm and Lodge Farm – from Nathaniel Soames in 1864 and Gate Hill Farm from Daniel Wilshin Soames in 1866. This made him the owner of 762 acres, spreading across a large part of Northwood.

THE METROPOLITAN RAILWAY

In 1886 the Metropolitan Railway was planning an extension from Harrow to Rickmansworth and needed a strip of land across the estate for the line and a station. Mr Carnegie met the company's requirements, dallied with the idea of offering land for building 'villas and better class housing', changed his mind and sold the whole estate in March 1887 before retiring to Scotland.

The line was declared open to traffic on 30th August 1887 and a half-hourly service from Aldgate to Rickmansworth was soon passing through the new station, providing, as a writer in the *Watford Observer* of 8th October said, 'new ground for the rambler'. The same writer noted that not a house could be seen from the station platform and remarked on the propensity of nightingales to sing in the neighbourhood. There were indeed only 62 cottages in Northwood in 1881, but great changes lay ahead.

90. Eastbury, built by David Carnegie 1857. The arms of the Earls of Southesk from whom he was descended can be seen on the front.

91. The new Ops Block at Coastal Command in 1961 before the house, which was being used as an Officers' Mess, was destroyed by fire.

DEVELOPING NORTHWOOD

The new owner of Carnegie's estate was Frank Murray Maxwell Hallowell Carew (1866-1943). He was just 21 and had married an actress (stage name Edith Chester) on the day before his purchase. Two sons were born, Reginald in 1888 and Roy in 1889, but the marriage ended in divorce in 1892. During the proceedings Mr Carew was described as 'a man of considerable independent means', a member of a firm of bill-brokers, Vaile & Carew, and more damagingly as 'a man of loose pursuits, who favoured the company of prize fighters, frequenters of race-courses and loose ladies who indulged in the midnight amusements of dancing saloons.'

He determined to develop Northwood. He laid out, but did not make up, roads which he named after himself, his sons and his wife. They were divided into building plots and houses were priced at £750 for a detached or £1300 for a semi-detached pair on Carew, Maxwell and Dene Roads; more cheaply, buyers were asked £400 for detached and £700 for a semi-detached pair on Chester and Murray Roads; even more cheaply, terraced cottages on the west side of Northwood High Street (called Half Mile Lane at the time) could be had for £120. Dene Road was originally Edith Road, the name changing after the divorce.

Ten sales were held between September 1887 and July 1891, usually in a marquee on the estate and preceded by a free lunch for limited numbers and by 1891 there were 115 houses, one shop and three public houses in Northwood. There were some large detached houses along Green Lane and Dene Road and several terraces of small cottages (much sought after 100 years later) in the High Street where small tradesmen and agricultural labourers lived. Mr Carew sold

92. Houses with dragons in Chester Road.

93. *Addison Road c1910.*

the remaining portions of the Middlesex part of the Eastbury estate to George Wieland in 1892, but the development started by him continued. By 1901 Northwood was a small town, with nearly 500 houses, 26 shops and a population of 2500.

THE URBAN POPULATION

The newcomers were largely families of professional men - solicitors, architects and superior tradesmen who owned high-class establishments in town and travelled daily to the City. They came to Northwood, wooed by advertisements extolling the delights of rural life, but after a short time found that they wanted street lighting, made-up roads and main drains. A rift appeared in the parish (although Northwood had become an ecclesiastical parish in 1854, it was still part of the civil parish of Ruislip) between the newly urban and old agricultural areas. The woods and reservoir created a physical division, but the greatest gap was social. Northwood had an orchestral society and golf club, while the people of Ruislip and Eastcote were still being entertained with lantern slides by the vicar.

When Ruislip Parish Council was set up in 1895, the nine councillors elected by a show of hands at a parish meeting held in Ruislip schoolroom included only one, Daniel Sydney Waterlow of the Thorns, Northwood who could be said to represent the newcomers. A five year struggle for a main drainage scheme convinced many Northwood inhabitants that the area needed urban powers if it were to run its own affairs efficiently, but a proposition that urban powers should be applied for was lost after a poll in May 1902. 'The result was declared... amid applause at Ruislip, but did not appear to cause much acclamation at Northwood'. The struggle was on.

94. *Tower Dene, designed by R.A. Briggs RIBA for Dr Dove.*

95. *Church Road c1920. Originally Half Mile Lane because it was half a mile from the bottom to Gate Hill Farm, the name changed when Emmanuel Church was built. The lower part where the shops are is now the High Street. The Northwood Picture House, opened in 1912, can be seen on the left.*

96. The Old Bell (now the RSPCA Shop, Delicatessen and St Martin's Book Shop) about 1910. Mr Moulder had taken over the bakery on the other side of the lychgate sometime between 1908-13 from Mr Laurance.

Ruislip Village at the Turn of this Century

A HAVEN OF RURAL REST

Around 1900 Ruislip was a quiet village, with its old church, a handful of small shops and three old-fashioned inns, the Bell, the Swan and the George. Peaceful winding lanes led to the equally attractive villages of Ickenham, Harefield and Pinner and to the reservoir (now Ruislip Lido). Visitors came in brakes, and cyclists often passed through, pausing for refreshment at the George which had a Cyclists' Touring Club sign outside. Motor cars were just beginning to make an appearance and in 1904 the Metropolitan Railway opened an extension from Harrow to Uxbridge, with a station at Ruislip, making the area accessible to walkers.

A *Daily Chronicle* Reporter in 1909 spoke of Ruislip as 'a haven of rural rest' where there was 'no sound more harsh than the thrush's song and the cuckoo's call' and praised its 'absolutely unspoiled antiquity' and the 'treasures hidden in odd corners'. He visited the Old Bell (now the RSPCA shop) and Mrs Wingfield, the hostess showed him the carved oak beam over the fireplace and the trefoil shaped niches above with their traces of colour. He noted that in spite of their nearness to London 'the Ruislip folk keep up a rural heartiness of their own.'

This was much in evidence in June 1913 when the flocks of visitors wending their way from the station towards the woods on a Saturday afternoon were arrested by the sight of an effigy of a woman clothed in a white dress with blue ribbons in the garden of the cottage next to the police station. At first it was thought to represent a suffragette, but a card round the neck announced that it was a woman who was 'a disgrace to the village and her sex' and was to be burnt. A crowd of over a hundred assembled to watch the firing, when petrol was poured over the figure and onlookers beat a tattoo on old pots and pans. Such a scene, which might have come out of a novel by Thomas Hardy, could not have taken place in sophisticated, urban Northwood and emphasises the growing difference between the two parts of the old parish.

97. Ruislip Village 1907. Advertisements, including one for the News of the World, *litter the walls and the new lychgate erected to commemorate the coronation of Edward VII can be seen.*

98. This sign was taken down when Crookall's shop became an estate agent's and was kept for a time in the Great Barn, but was unfortunately taken away with rubbish about1980.

SHOPS AND INNS

There was a long tradition of the licensee at the George running a butcher's shop from a hut built to one side of the inn. J.A. Thurkettle at the beginning of the century was the last to do so, as the businesses became separated when Mr Crookall took over the butcher's and Alex Hoar, the George, about 1906. Mr Crookall, who had a Royal Warrant above his door for supplying the Dowager Queen of Sweden during her residence at Highgrove, expanded into the next door cottage on the corner of the High Street.

The George, which first appears in the licensed victuallers records in 1762, was a popular place of resort under Mr Hoar and had an assembly room at the back. Although there was a bowling green and tea gardens for trippers, Cannon Breweries, the owners wanted a smarter, more up-to-date road house in the 1930s, more in keeping with the suburb that Ruislip had then become. The present George (now a Harvester Restaurant) was constructed behind the original building in 1939 and for a short time the two Georges stood together.

The Old Bell at the end of the High Street extended further north than it does today. The northern end was a cottage. Two bays of the building were demolished in 1927 when the corner was widened to ease traffic problems. The wing next to the lych gate has finely moulded joists as well as a beautiful fireplace and was clearly an important house in the 16th century. By 1748 it was licensed and 18th-century Vestry meetings were often adjourned 'to the sign of the One Bell'. The house surrendered its licence in 1931 and is now the RSPCA shop. When antiques were sold there in the 1940s and 50s, Queen Mary used to visit it.

A baker and confectioner, Mr Laurance, lived in the old timber-framed house on the other side of the lych-

99. The George soon after 1907 when Alex Hoar took over the licence. Large tea gardens and good accommodation for cyclists are being advertised.

THE
GEORGE
HOTEL.
ALEX. H. HOAR.
ACCOMMODATION FOR
CYCLISTS & TOURISTS
& STANMORE.
LONDON.
NOTICE
STATION
RUISLIP

100. Police Sergeant Dunsford standing outside the second Police Station about 1913.

gate and there was a post office and stores on the opposite side of the road. By 1895 Mr H. V. Puddick was postmaster and Mrs Riddle, widow of the former postmaster, sold drapery, haberdashery, newspapers, stationery, teas and refreshments.

Looking down the High Street stood two cottages. The one by the entrance to Manor Farm became well known as Hailey's and was the Post Office from 1907-27. The first telephone exchange was there too. Mr Hailey also sold greengrocery and other provisions and was a keen photographer.

The third village inn, the Swan, is the only one still functioning. The south wing has a king-post roof and the building belonged to John Walleston in the mid-16th century.

RUISLIP POLICE STATION

Ruislip's first police sergeants, part of the Metropolitan Police Force, were mounted and from 1845 lived at a cottage in Ickenham Road on the edge of the Park Estate. It was later called Byeway Cottage and demolished in 1926. In 1869 the police rented a house on the east side of the High Street from Richard Ewer of Hill Farm. From its appearance it was an early Victorian house, inhabited by a commercial traveller in the 1850s. There was a stable at the back where the police kept a hand ambulance and later their cycles. After 1873, when the police purchased the copyhold, the house was converted to provide living accommodation for a sergeant or inspector and his family, as well as a charge room, parade room and cells.

There were also police constables living in the village. In 1891 William French and his family lived at Laurel Cottage (next to the Laurels) in Sharps Lane and Constable John Gittins, a mounted policeman, lodged with them. Other members of the Ruislip force included a constable at Ruislip Common, two at Northwood, an acting-sergeant and two constables at Eastcote, a sergeant and four constables at Pinner and one at Ickenham. Northwood got a police station of its own in 1910.

The High Street Police Station was in use until 1961, when a new building erected on land purchased at a Park House sale way back in 1906, was opened.

101. Mrs Riddle and her daughters outside her shop next to Crookall's, probably at the time of George V's coronation in 1911. The Daily Mirror *was searching for the fattest woman in the world.*

102. *Queen Mary at the church after visiting the antique shop at the former Old Bell in April 1950. She is accompanied by the vicar, the Revd E.C. Mortimer, with Mr Fawcett the curate behind.*

THE VILLAGE PUMP

The old farmhouses all over the parish and the estate cottages built by landowners like Lawrance James Baker of Haydon Hall, had their own wells, but many cottagers had to rely upon ponds for their water supply. A public well was sunk at the junction of High Street and Bury Street, right in the centre of Ruislip in 1864 and a pump was erected on top. Mr Charles Page of Uxbridge, dug down the first 15 feet, then bored a further 90¾ feet through the London Clay, the Reading Beds and finally 30 feet into the chalk. The water rose to the surface and there was always a good supply. Shallower wells that did not go into the chalk sometimes dried up during droughts.

The summer of 1898 was one of the driest on record and the want of water was sorely felt in Ruislip, but the 'boiling springs' in the moors (now the Pinn Fields) between Ruislip and Eastcote never failed to supply an abundance of water. The vicar, Mr Marsh-Everett, thought that an effort ought to be made by the Parish or District Council to utilise it. The Colne Valley Water Company (founded 1873) already sup-

103. *The Swan stands on the corner of Park Lane, which was sometimes called Swan Alley and is now the Oaks. The photograph shows the narrow lane and the wall surrounding Park House grounds, just when Mrs Gooderson's shop was being demolished in 1930.*

104. The pump sunk in 1864 was the focal point of village gossip.

105. A view down the High Street towards Hailey's and Mrs Bray's sweet shop. The Swan, like the Old Bell a Salter's Brewery house, is on the left. Salter's was later taken over by Cannon's Brewery.

106. Cissy Bell, Lucy Allen and their grandfather Bell outside Park Lane Cottages. The back of the Swan is in the centre of the picture and directly across the road can be seen the gardens of the cottages where the effigy of a woman was burnt in 1913.

107. A load of hay passing the George. On the left is Crookall's butcher's shop with the sign, saying that he was patronised by the Dowager Queen of Sweden, above the door.

108. The Warrender Institute given by Eleanor Warrender in 1907. Later, the fire station stood on the site.

109. Perhaps this picture was taken in or shortly after 1907, when this old house on the corner of Park Lane had ceased to be the Post Office, for it appears to be empty. Mrs Gooderson started trading there a few years later. Cissy Bell is sitting on the bench outside the Swan.

plied the new houses in Northwood from wells near Watford and had extended a main to Eastcote in 1888, but wanted a guaranteed amount of £45 per annum before providing piped water to Ruislip. Probably because of the drought the Parish Council concluded negotiations rapidly and the supply was laid on in 1899. Tile Kilns had to wait until 1903 for mains water.

ENTERTAINMENT

There were plenty of activities to fill the men's limited leisure time. The public houses always provided a cosy refuge from home life and the Warrender Institute with its gramophone and newspapers could be a background for more intellectual pursuits. The vicar was very musical and organised many concerts and Penny Readings, attended by both men and women and usually held in the School Room. He sometimes had occasion to reprimand the young men, however, for not politely listening to the lecturer on a lantern slide evening. The vicar's wife held a Mothers' Meeting every Wednesday afternoon.

Ruislip had a cricket club from about 1872 and home matches were played on a meadow adjoining Manor Farm. From 1906 Ruislip Sports Day (see pages 80-81) was held on the same meadow (now St Martin's Approach). The photographs and reminiscences suggest that the sports were lighthearted, including an egg and spoon race, climbing a slippery pole and catching a greased pig. The afternoon always began with a fancy dress parade; there were roundabouts and swingboats and other attributes of a fair. The sports were held in August and quite separate from Ruislip Fair which was held on Ascension Day and attended by gypsies and stallholders.

The local paper for 1892 complained that the fair was dying out and a mere vestige of its former self, with only one stall, but if that were true for that year, the fair revived and carried on even after the First World War and finally petered out in the late 1920s.

110. The egg-and-spoon race at Ruislip Sports Day in 1908.

111. The Fancy Dress event at Ruislip Sports Day 1906.

112. Ruislip Village. The little girls on the extreme left are leaning against the fence of a house called The Oaks, the home of Mr W. J. Collins. It was one of the earliest houses built on the Park estate.

113. Ticket to Ruislip Sports 1921.

114. Advertisements for various Ruislip businesses.

RUISLIP SPORTS. Affiliated to the A.A.A.

PRESIDENT: REV. W. A. G. GRAY.

ADMIT BEARER to the

Annual Sports & Old English Fair

TO BE HELD IN THE

MANOR FIELD, RUISLIP,

(By kind permission of R. EWER Esq.

On SATURDAY, AUGUST 6th, 1921.

COMMENCING AT 1.30 P.M.

ADMISSION 1/3; if purchased before the day, 9d.

(Including Tax)

H. GALLOP,

(Late COX),

Builder, Undertaker, &c.

EASTCOTE.

Books for selection of Wall Papers kept during the Season

Funerals to suit all Classes Personally Attended

"Black Horse," Eastcote.

R. Husbands, Proprietor

WINE AND SPIRIT MERCHANT.

Good Accommodation for Cyclists.

F. TAPPING,

COACH BUILDER & GENERAL SMITH

EASTCOTE.

ICE BOATS BUILT TO ORDER

W. J. RIDDLE,

COACH AND CART BUILDER,

RICK AND FRUIT LADDER MAKER,

Draper, Grocer, Corn, Coal and General Provision Merchant,

Post Office, Stamp Office, Money Order & Savings' Bank,

RUISLIP.

Stationery, Turps, Oils, &c. Agent for the Post Office Teas.

CARTS and VANS of every Description Built to Order.

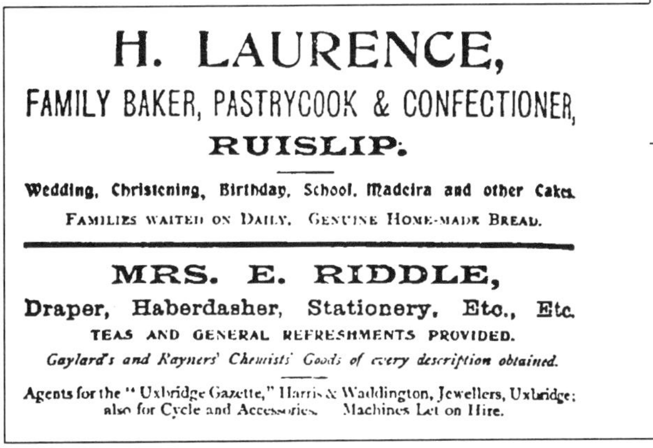

H. LAURENCE,

FAMILY BAKER, PASTRYCOOK & CONFECTIONER,

RUISLIP.

Wedding, Christening, Birthday, School, Madeira and other Cakes.

FAMILIES WAITED ON DAILY. GENUINE HOME-MADE BREAD.

MRS. E. RIDDLE,

Draper, Haberdasher, Stationery, Etc., Etc.

TEAS AND GENERAL REFRESHMENTS PROVIDED.

Gaylard's and Kayners' Chemists' Goods of every description obtained.

Agents for the "Uxbridge Gazette," Harris & Waddington, Jewellers, Uxbridge; also for Cycle and Accessories. Machines Let on Hire.

Tea Gardens and Trippers

As soon as Ruislip Station opened on 4 July 1904 ramblers were able to join the cyclists who had been making Ruislip Reservoir the object of their outings for some years. They poured out of London in their thousands, seeking fresh air and country delights and all panting for refreshment after their exertions. It was provided in abundance in many cottage gardens which were thrown open to trippers, usually on a small scale, by cottagers' wives assisted by daughters and nieces. James Bunce had a pleasant orchard and splendid greenhouse at Bury Farm. He was listed as a greengrocer in street directories at the turn of the century, but during the summer he set out trestle tables and chairs under his fruit trees and his daughter and granddaughter served teas.

Down on the High Street, Mrs Riddle advertised a 'tea-garden' and so did Mr Hoar at the George. Mrs Weedon at Field End Farm just south of the station was willing to turn her hand to providing teas on any fine day.

116. James Bunce and his granddaughter Rose in the orchard at Bury Farm.

THE POPLARS AND KING'S END FARM

A far more commercially organised tea-garden was opened by George Thomas Weedon at the Poplars, on the corner of Ruislip High Street and Ickenham Road. The Poplars was a pretty Georgian house built in 1774 by a carpenter, George King, suitable for a professional man or small tradesman. Peter Elige, a surgeon, bought it in 1790 and lived there until his death about 1808. Daniel Barrenger carried on his business as wheelwright and undertaker there in the middle of

115. Bury Farm, which incorporates the wall of a medieval hall. The central hearth is still in position beneath the floorboards.

117. The Poplars on the corner of the High Street and Ickenham Road opened as a Tea Garden in June 1906.

118. The sports field at the Poplars.

119. George Weedon on the right with his staff at the Poplars. The waitresses wear their bunches of flowers; Rose is third from the left in the middle row.

the century. The house became part of Ruislip Park and was acquired by Mr Weedon at the break up of the estate.

He was a man with an entrepreneurial flair, advertising far and wide and attracting vast crowds to his gardens during those long Edwardian summer afternoons - as many as 3000 trippers are said to have been served in a single day. The local girls employed as waitresses were given flower names and wore bunches of artificial flowers to match, pinned to their aprons. Souvenirs in the shape of tea-pots, cream jugs and sugar basins, decorated with pictures of the house, sold in enormous numbers, and postcards and sheet music of the specially written Poplars' Waltz were also available. The chorus of the song on which the waltz was based went:

And we spend the day with Rose you see
At the Poplars where sweet Bluebell serves the tea,
And Lily's white hand brings cakes and jam
And don't we enjoy Miss Pansy's cold lamb!
The jellies and custard by Poppy and May
And the cream brought by Daisy is sweet as hay.
It's a very short distance by rail on the "Met"
And at the gate you'll find waiting Sweet Violet.

George Weedon also owned King's End Farm at the junction of Ickenham Road and Sharps Lane. He turned the fields into the Poplars Sports Fields, with cricket pitches, swing boats, donkey rides and coconut shies, and advertised it as 'an ideal place for School Treats and large Pleasure Parties' – 1500 people could be seated in permanent buildings at one sitting. Children's teas cost sixpence and adults' ninepence; no intoxicants were sold, which encouraged Sunday School parties, but the White Bear was just across the road for those who could not stay the course without the help of something stronger than tea. An 18-hole golf course was formed at King's End Farm, which was the start of the present Ruislip Golf Club.

During the 1920s the lanes and fields through which the ramblers and day-trippers had wandered, began to be built up and much more development was in prospect. The Poplars was demolished in 1929 to make way for shops, but King's End Farm remained and was used as the Club House of the golf course from 1939 until 1951. Houses were then built on the site and a new Club House erected farther down the road.

120. *A Donkey Derby at King's End Farm.*

121. *Advertisement for the pleasures of King's End Farm.*

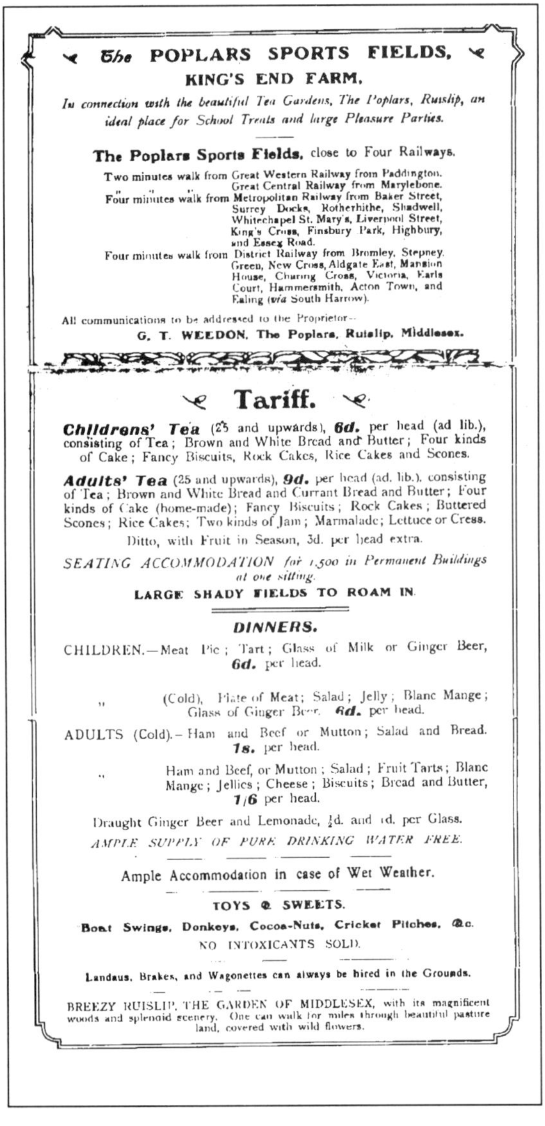

The POPLARS SPORTS FIELDS,

KING'S END FARM,

In connection with the beautiful Tea Gardens, The Poplars, Ruislip, an ideal place for School Treats and large Pleasure Parties.

The Poplars Sports Fields, close to Four Railways.

Two minutes walk from Great Western Railway from Paddington.
" " " Great Central Railway from Marylebone.
Four minutes walk from Metropolitan Railway from Baker Street, Surrey Docks, Rotherhithe, Shadwell, Whitechapel St. Mary's, Liverpool Street, King's Cross, Finsbury Park, Highbury, and Essex Road.
Four minutes walk from District Railway from Bromley, Stepney Green, New Cross, Aldgate East, Mansion House, Charing Cross, Victoria, Earls Court, Hammersmith, Acton Town, and Ealing (*via* South Harrow).

All communications to be addressed to the Proprietor—

G. T. WEEDON, The Poplars, Ruislip, Middlesex.

Tariff.

Childrens' Tea (25 and upwards), ***6d.*** per head (ad lib.), consisting of Tea; Brown and White Bread and Butter; Four kinds of Cake; Fancy Biscuits, Rock Cakes, Rice Cakes and Scones.

Adults' Tea (25 and upwards), ***9d.*** per head (ad. lib.), consisting of Tea; Brown and White Bread and Currant Bread and Butter; Four kinds of Cake (home-made); Fancy Biscuits; Rock Cakes; Buttered Scones; Rice Cakes; Two kinds of Jam; Marmalade; Lettuce or Cress.

Ditto, with Fruit in Season, 3d. per head extra.

SEATING ACCOMMODATION for 1,500 in Permanent Buildings at one sitting.

LARGE SHADY FIELDS TO ROAM IN.

DINNERS.

CHILDREN.—Meat Pie; Tart; Glass of Milk or Ginger Beer, ***6d.*** per head.

" (Cold), Plate of Meat; Salad; Jelly; Blanc Mange; Glass of Ginger Beer. ***6d.*** per head.

ADULTS (Cold).—Ham and Beef or Mutton; Salad and Bread. ***1s.*** per head.

" Ham and Beef, or Mutton; Salad; Fruit Tarts; Blanc Mange; Jellies; Cheese; Biscuits; Bread and Butter, ***1/6*** per head.

Draught Ginger Beer and Lemonade, ½d. and 1d. per Glass.

AMPLE SUPPLY OF PURE DRINKING WATER FREE.

Ample Accommodation in case of Wet Weather.

TOYS & SWEETS.

Boat Swings, Donkeys, Cocoa-Nuts, Cricket Pitches, &c.

NO INTOXICANTS SOLD.

Landaus, Brakes, and Wagonettes can always be hired in the Grounds.

BREEZY RUISLIP, THE GARDEN OF MIDDLESEX, with its magnificent woods and splendid scenery. One can walk for miles through beautiful pasture land, covered with wild flowers.

THE ORCHARD BUNGALOW

Yet another catering establishment opened in Ickenham Road, at the corner of Sharps Lane (very close to King's End Farm) soon after the opening of the station. Albert Cross put up a low building with a veranda in what had been the orchard of the Park estate and called it the Orchard Bungalow. Rustic tables and chairs were scattered under the trees and teas were served. Mr and Mrs R. Raymont made it a popular rendezvous and with the success of the venture the bungalow was given another storey.

After the Raymonts left the place was run as a hotel, which acquired a slightly dubious reputation, as couples who could not afford Brighton were thought to spend naughty weekends there. From 1933 until about 1971 it was run as a high-class restaurant by Ansells and it is now a Beefeater Steak House. Mr Ansell had been head waiter at Rule's in Maiden Lane, Covent Garden.

THE SHIP, JOEL STREET

The Ship in Joel Street was the County Quarters for the Elgin, Kensal Rise and Paddington Cycling Clubs at the beginning of the century and the London Scottish Volunteers (Volunteers became Territorials in 1908) also used it, marching out from their HQ in Buckingham Palace Road. About 1908 the landlord Harry Sylvester produced a brochure extolling the virtues of his pub as a place of accessible entertainment for walkers and strollers as well as the fit and hearty soldiery. He suggested a pleasant route from Pinner Station along footpaths over Cuckoo Hill, which are still walkable today. Eastcote Halt opened in 1906, but was 1½ miles away.

At the back of the Ship stood a pavilion with a veranda, looking rather similar to the Orchard Bungalow, where dances and concerts were held. Outside were swings, and sixpenny teas and two-shilling dinners were on offer. The pavilion has disappeared within the last ten years, but the Ship is still a bustling public house, though no longer 'miles out in the country'. A sign saying 'Sedgwick's Watford Stout, Ales and Porter' can still be faintly discerned on the side wall.

THE PAVILION

Arthur Baily, catering manager at the Regent Street Polytechnic bought a house standing in fields a short distance south of Eastcote Halt and built a pavilion for a tea-room in the grounds. The gardens were laid out and swing boats, see-saws and a troupe of donkeys installed for the delight of child visitors. As he was a member of the Salvation Army he hoped to encourage church groups and charitable organisations to bring children out from the East End and inner London, to enjoy a day in the country. The venture was wildly

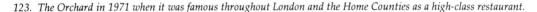

122. The Orchard Bungalow opened at Easter 1905. Winnifred Raymont, daughter of the proprietors, sits at a table reading.

123. The Orchard in 1971 when it was famous throughout London and the Home Counties as a high-class restaurant.

successful and after the First World War cheap train tickets were issued to Eastcote and special trains ran on bank holidays, when queues stretched down Field End Road, waiting to get into the grounds. Organisations like the Salvation Army had special days there.

The Pavilion was not open on Sundays and did not serve alcohol, so the astute landlord of the Ship had his own hostelry strategically advertised. The Pavilion closed at the end of the summer, but shooting parties came in the autumn for the pheasants and also to shoot clay pigeons at the range nearby (the Clay Pigeon public house is now on the site).

Mr Baily died aged 56 in 1930 and the business was continued by the manager, C.W. Hester. For the first time music and dancing were introduced and tea dances were very popular, but Eastcote was developing and the land was wanted for building. In 1935 it was sold to Davis Estates and today only Pavilion Way reminds us those past occasions.

124. London children heading for the Pavilion from Eastcote Station.

125. Mr and Mrs Reynolds outside the Ship in the 1920s. The Cyclists' Touring Club sign can be seen near the door.

126. Hockey being played at the Eastcote Pavilion.

Suburban Inroads

RUISLIP-NORTHWOOD URBAN DISTRICT COUNCIL

The people of Northwood did not give up the struggle for urban powers after their defeat in 1902. The newcomers had much stronger representation on the Parish Council than had been the case in 1895, having five of the nine seats, and the forward thinking Clerk to the Council, Edward R. Abbott and the Chairman, Frank M. Elgood, the architect were both from Northwood.

The threat that Northwood should become an urban district on its own account and the silver tongue of the Reverend W.A.G. Gray, who had succeeded Mr Marsh-Everett as vicar in 1900, swayed a parish meeting held on 28th October 1903 and Ruislip-Northwood Urban District Council came into being on 30th September 1904. Mr Abbott was appointed clerk at £100 per annum, a position he retained until 1931. Three committees were established: Finance and General Purposes; Public Health, Buildings and Sewerage; and Highways. Mr Walter Louis Carr of Wakefield was appointed Sanitary Inspector and Dr L.W. Hignett of Northwood became Medical Officer of Health.

128. Revd W.A.G. Gray, Vicar of Ruislip (1900-23) 'speaking disarmingly suggested to his audience that they would all quickly admit that the agricultural mind did not travel quite so quickly, and did not come to a conclusion quite so promptly as the city or business mind did, but he did not know that it was not in the end likely to come to a right conclusion.'

127. The RNUDC Highways Department at work c1907.

129. Eastcote Station photographed in February 1933.

130. Ruislip Manor Station in 1933.

131. *The official opening train at Ruislip, 30 June 1904. The station opened to the public on the 4 July, and the line was electrified on 1 January the following year.*

PLANNING

Perhaps the main concern of the Council was to ensure that the new urban district developed along pleasant residential lines. Mr Elgood and Mr Abbott were particularly influenced by the Garden Suburb movement and were in close contact with Raymond Unwin and other architects working on Hampstead Garden Suburb which began in 1906. When the movement culminated in the Housing and Town Planning Act, December 1909, they were quick to prompt their fellow councillors to adopt a scheme to enable them to control the style and quality of future developments. Their peers probably needed little persuading as they thought poorly of 'the badly-arranged and closely-packed working-class area near Northwood Station' and were appalled at some of the new developments already under way, particularly in Eastcote and South Ruislip.

It was important to move quickly, because the advent of more railway stations made development inevitable. Ruislip Station opened on 4th July 1904, the same day as the line itself, followed by a halt at Eastcote in May 1906. The Great Eastern and Great Central Joint Committee opened a station called Ruislip and Ickenham (now West Ruislip) in 1906 and Northolt Junction (now South Ruislip) in 1908.

The major landowner around Ruislip Station was King's College. Eastcote Halt lay between Walter Morford's Field End House Farm lands and Ralph Hawtrey Deane's land and Northolt Junction was on Bourne Farm, another of Mr Deane's properties. The three landowners proceeded in slightly different ways.

DEVELOPMENTS AT EASTCOTE AND SOUTH RUISLIP

The British Freehold Investment Syndicate acquired part of Field End House Farm in 1909 and began developing it by dividing the land into small plots which were sold individually or in groups at public sales. Brochures with pretty pictures of the 'village' of Eastcote encouraged buyers to invest in land - £3 down could secure any plot and the balance could be paid off at 10 shillings a month. Duplex drainage, electric light and park-like roads were promised to the prospective buyer.The roads laid out became Lime Grove, the west side of Hawthorn Avenue, Myrtle Avenue, Acacia Avenue and Elm Avenue. In a few months 650 plots were sold at an average price of £50 and this encouraged the Syndicate to parcel out land south of the railway line (Beech Avenue, Oak Grove and the eastern end of Linden Avenue), in the same way.

Ralph Hawtrey Deane sold two of the Bourne Farm fields to British Freehold in August 1910 and more land adjoining in November 1911. The Council was alarmed. There was no control over the use of the land and rather flimsy bungalows or even mere sheds

132. Estate agents' offices in wooden huts appeared near all the new stations. Noel Moore stands outside his father's hut c1926, on the King's End side of Ruislip Station bridge.

133. Early developments on the Park Estate, showing houses in Manor Road.

were being built by owners with little capital: 'Shanty-towns' seemed to be in danger of mushrooming in Eastcote and South Ruislip. Another point deplored by the authorities was that the roads as laid out and surrounded by farm land, were nearly all cul-de-sacs. The six roads south of the railway had only one narrow bridge approach (now Oak Grove) and councillors thought that this was 'just the kind of thing they ought to prevent occurring'. In May 1910 they decided to adopt a Town Plan.

KING'S COLLEGE AS DEVELOPERS

Had all landowners behaved as responsibly as King's College there might have been less anxiety. When the College began to develop its demesne land it attempted to control the quality of buildings rather as Mr Carew had done in Northwood twenty years earlier.

Withicrofts (or Withycuts/Widdicuts), the old enclosed pasture bounded by Wood Lane, Ickenham Road and the High Street was advertised for letting on building leases in 1903 and a new road called King's End Avenue (now King's End) from the station to Great King's End was begun in 1905. Frederick Herbert Mansford FRIBA (1871-1946) built the first two houses, now 13 and 15. To meet the College's requirements for imposing housing, he made the semi-detached pair look as much like a single house as possible, adding wings to enhance their appearance. The Mansfords moved into No 15 in 1907, calling it Walden after the book by the philosopher, Henry Thoreau, which described a simple life passed in idyllic solitude. The same name had been used for a house in Northwood a few years earlier and perhaps exemplified the view of rural Middlesex held by newcomers from inner London.

By 1909 the College was contemplating a planning scheme for its own estate which formed the central portion of the urban district.

134. 'The Daily Mail Cottage' was re-erected at the bottom of King's End after its first appearance at the Ideal Homes Exhibition at Olympia. Mr Dicky, who was in films, and his family lived there until 1910. It was demolished despite local objections in the late 1930s to make way for shops.

THE TOWN PLAN

A competition for the layout of the King's College estate was won by Messrs A. & J. Soutar of Wandsworth. Their plan owed more to geometry than the levels and contours of the parish of Ruislip. A main axial road ran north-south, right through the woods to South Ruislip with diagonal roads giving access to outlying portions; some small bands of Copse Wood and Park Wood were to be left as public open space, just enough to form a pleasing backdrop to the houses, and the golf course at Northwood (founded 1891) was to remain as a magnet for the 'right type' of resident.

Socially the estate was graded from north to south with large houses at low density (three to the acre in Copse Wood and four and a half to the acre in Park Wood). Medium-sized houses (eight to the acre) and shops were planned between the woods and the railway, while to the south smaller houses (10 to the acre could be built and some land was made available for industrial purposes. Six shopping areas were envisaged about the axial road, the main one being at the junction of Eastcote Road and the new road at Windmill Hill, where public buildings were to adorn the summit. The Reservoir and Pinn were both intended to become recreational areas with aquatic sports on the one and ornamental gardens alongside the other.

Messrs Soutar envisaged 7,642 houses being built on the estate eventually, with 35,000 residents, by which time the entire urban district was expected to have a population of about 70,000. In the event this was a reasonably accurate estimate, for when the Ruislip-Northwood Urban District Council became part of the Borough of Hillingdon in 1964, the population had reached 75,000. By 1991 it had fallen to 70,426.

Many features of Soutar's plan were excellent: low-density housing (nowhere more than 10 to the acre) good-sized gardens, landscaped streets and space for churches, schools and public amenities. But there was a complete disregard for every ancient feature except St Martin's church and for the woodland which was to be almost totally destroyed. Manor Farm with the Great Barn and other farm buildings were to be torn down to give place to houses and workshops and the 16th-century buildings at the end of the High Street (admittedly in a poor state at that time) were also to be lost.

The Ruislip-Northwood Town Planning Scheme received final approval in September 1914 and its provisions governed all development until it was abrogated by the Town and Country Planning Act of 1947.

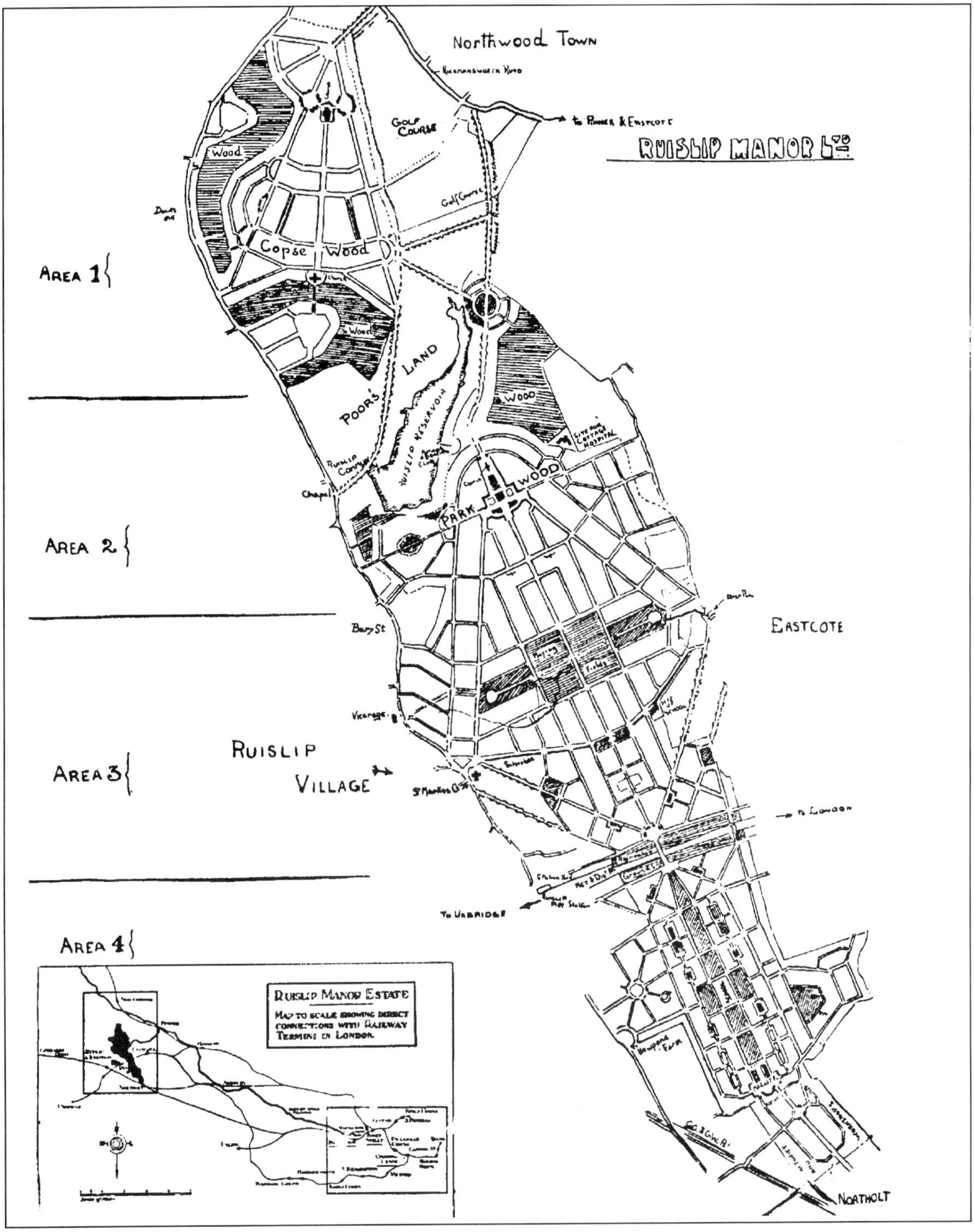

135. A. & J. Soutar's winning planning scheme for the King's College demesne land.

136. The first new shops on the High Street were erected about 1912 – Blackwell's ironmonger's, the International Stores, Evans' pharmacy, Tapscott fancy goods, a greengrocer's, the Cabin sweets and Saul's the butcher.

137. The earliest shops at South Ruislip built about 1912. Hundred Acres Farm Dairy is on the left. The farm was in West End Road opposite the end of Station Approach.

Modest Housing

RUISLIP MANOR COTTAGE SOCIETY

In his account of the Ruislip Scheme in *Town Planning in Practice* Alderman Thompson stated that architects believed that the indiscriminate intermixing of large and small houses was inadmissable, but that a judicious sprinkling of medium-sized houses among large ones would not depreciate values. He also thought it necessary to provide 'specific areas near large houses for housing the working classes employed in connection therewith' – charladies, gardeners, etc.

With this provision in mind a subsidiary company called the Ruislip Manor Cottage Society Ltd was registered in October 1911. Its purpose was to take up land to build small houses and cottages for either selling or letting. It had the same bankers, auditors and registered office as Ruislip Manor Ltd, and the same architects, A. & J. Soutar. Most of the members of the Board were local men and women and included George Weedon of the Poplars and F.H. Mansford of Walden.

The aim of the Society was to build well-designed and attractive cottages for 'persons in receipt of moderate or small salaries and wages', while encouraging such people to be thrifty and careful tenants by making provision for profit sharing tenancies. Small houses were to be rented at six shillings to 15 shillings per

139. (Top) The first houses built for the Ruislip Manor Cottage Society by Bunney & Makins, 1911.

140. (Centre) Cottages in Green Walk completed in 1919.

138. A pre-1914 picture showing Windmill Way and Priory Close in the distance.

week and tenants, who would be obliged to invest a minimum of £5 in the Society, would share in the surplus profits. A rent-purchase scheme was also contemplated. For a down payment of £25-£50 plus an annual payment equal to the rental value, ownership could be achieved within 15-20 years.

Land was conveyed freehold to the Cottage Society by Ruislip Manor Ltd with roads, sewers and open spaces ready made. The main sphere of operations was between Eastcote Road, Windmill Hill and the new Ruislip Manor Halt, but two smaller areas were also acquired, one between Fore Street and Park Wood (now Coteford Close) and the other at Northwood (Chestnut Avenue).

Only Manor Way, Windmill Way and Park Way were constructed before the First World War. The first two houses erected at the corner of Eastcote Road and Manor Way were designed by architects Bunney & Makins, and are still extremely attractive. They are built of grey and brown Tring bricks, have oak half timbering and soft red hanging tiles. Their jettied upper storey, oak doors with iron strapping and decorative chimneys typify the 'Elizabethan' style favoured in garden suburbs, and seen here at its best, built with quality materials and good workmanship. What is so ironical is that the architects who strove to imitate 16th-century styles, viewed the proposed destruction of genuine Tudor buildings on the High Street and at Manor Farm with equanimity.

Some rooms in one of the pairs were set aside as offices for the Society and indeed still fulfil that purpose. Twelve more houses built in Manor Way in 1911 are grouped around a large green (four pairs and a group of four) and were designed by different architects, H.A. Welch, A. & J. Soutar and Courtenay M. Crickmer. These houses, let at 10 or 11 shillings a week, all had bathrooms and inside WCs and three bedrooms, and most had tool sheds for the expected artisan tenants.

A similar development was begun in Windmill Way of fourteen houses, designed by Cecil H. Hignett around a green. He specified local multi-coloured bricks, Norfolk pantile roofs and ivory-white woodwork. These slightly simpler houses did not have bathrooms, but had a bath as well as sinks and washing boilers in the sculleries. The rents varied from six shillings and sixpence to eight shillings and sixpence a week.

The outbreak of war in 1914 put an immediate end to building, leaving the trucks of bricks and sand and the light railway laid by the contractor from Ruislip Station sidings as a playground for small boys. Work

141. On both pages, advertisements and copy designed to attract newcomers to suburban Ruislip.

NORTHWOOD

Pinner Hill Farm Estate

Situated within 5 minutes of New Metro. Railway Station, now being built at Joel Street, Northwood. Coach and Bus routes pass the Estate. Journey to Baker Street on Metro. Railway is 22 minutes.

Exceedingly well-built Houses & Bungalows in a delightful picturesque setting, have been built for the buyer who wants

"Something Different"

THE ELEVATION IS ORIGINAL AND PLEASING

The rooms are of a comfortable size—WELL LIGHTED AND COSY

THE THIRD BEDROOM is REALLY "A" Bedroom !

KITCHENETTE has Tiled walls and floors, is fitted with independent boiler for domestic hot-water supply, and the heating of radiators which are fitted in Hall and best Bedrooms.

BATH ROOM is Tiled and fitted with Tiled-in Square Bath or open Bath to choice. Separate W.C.

Large range of unique designs in Fire Places and Mantelpieces for Purchasers' choice. Decorative colours to Tenants' selection. Tastefully designed Lead-lights are fitted to Casement Sashes.
Plaster Panelled Ceiling and Cornices to Reception Rooms and Best Bedrooms. Dining Room fitted with C. & C. Gas and Fuel Fireplaces: Gaslighted Fuel Fires in five minutes.

We do not build Palaces—but REAL HOMES

Prices range from: { **BUNGALOWS £625 to £850**
HOUSES - - £795 to £825

SMALL DEPOSIT SECURES

SOUTH RUISLIP (Middlesex)

THIS is a very delightful modern residential settlement adjacent to Ruislip and in close proximity to Northolt, Ealing, Harrow, etc.

Its elevation (standing, as it does, at an altitude of about 120 to 140 feet above sea-level), with a subsoil of loam, surrounded by a beautiful stretch of open country, free from anything suggestive of overcrowding, give to this charming spot an inestimable value for residential purposes, and for those who desire fresh, pure air, bracing climate and rural peace it can be highly recommended.

The most remarkable asset to this desirable district is the fact that it is but 26 minutes by train from London. The station serving South Ruislip is Northolt Junction, which is reached either from Marylebone (L.N.E.R.) or Paddington (G.W.R.), with a frequent and very good service of trains. Thus the very heart of the great metropolis is within easy access, and any London theatre can be comfortably reached in 35 minutes.

There are the magnificent shopping areas of Harrow and Ealing within ten minutes and Ruislip (five minutes). Together with this are every form of indoor and outdoor sports and amusements—Wembley Stadium for greyhound racing, speedway and football is 15 minutes distance—whilst Northolt Park, with its beautiful racecourse, is within five minutes of South Ruislip.

began again in 1919, but less was achieved by the Cottage Society than had been envisaged. Only four houses were built at Eastcote, the rest of Coteford Close being sold to the Council for council housing, and 18 cottages were built in Chestnut Avenue, Northwood in 1926. Green Walk and Manor Close were built in Ruislip, but the remaining area of Windmill Hill was sold to private developers.

Plans for a public hall on the corner of Manor Way and Midcroft and the fine shopping centre on Windmill Hill did not materialise and the Society was not successful in encouraging the sale of its houses to tenants - only one house on Manor Way was sold and the rest are still rented. In many respects, however, the Society was and still is highly successful. It built cottages of great charm and placed them in green spaces which still delight the eye and it set a high standard for the Council to aspire to when it, too started providing accommodation for the working classes.

COUNCIL HOUSES

Ruislip-Northwood Urban District Council took its responsibilty to increase the number of good quality houses for the working classes seriously and began building in Reservoir Road and Field Way, Ruislip; Coteford Close, Eastcote and Pinner Road, Northwood, immediately after the First World War. By 1939, 445 houses had been built, all in a cottage style and of a suitable brick which fitted the local landscape. They are attractive, but lack some of the imaginative detailing of the Cottage Society's dwellings. Post-war council estates are bleaker and less in sympathy with their surroundings.

THE MANOR HOMES

Large-scale estate development in which one builder developed many acres became more commonplace in the 1930s. Many of the estates consisted of semi-detached houses with a sprinkling of detached ones and were bought by the middle-classes, but George Ball's Manor Homes were built in short terraces and aimed at the working man who wanted to become a homeowner. They sold from £450.

The Manor Homes built between 1933 and 1939 now form the area called Ruislip Manor. King's College sold George Ball 186 acres south of the railway where he intended to build 2,322 houses. In order to have space for a school (Lady Bankes Primary School) he agreed to forego 50 houses in 1934 and reduced the number of houses by a further 34 in 1935 in return for permission to put up a church (St Paul's) and a public house (the Black Bull). Land near the Yeading Brook was set aside as open space in 1937.

The distinctive style of the George Ball houses made little pretence to 'olde worlde' charm, apart

142. *Most of the thirties' housing was traditional Tudorbethan in style, but three houses by Connell, Ward & Lucas, standing in Park Avenue, built in 1936 strike a modernistic note.*

143. *Reservoir Road – the first houses built by RNUDC overlooking the reservoir.*

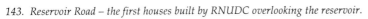

144. People living in caravans, usually in Breakspear Road, appear in Victorian censuses, and gypsies still live in the Ruislip area. This photograph was taken in 1960.

145. The Drag Hunt meeting outside the Plough, Bury Street in 1934. Having been attracted to Ruislip, 'London's healthiest suburb', the middle classes were pleased to find rural pursuits on their doorstep.

from timbered gables. The small houses (many had only two bedrooms) are built along the functional lines of the 1930s: the Crittall windows in particular epitomise the period, but these are becoming a rarity as most of them have been replaced in recent years.

The Manor Homes were advertised with great verve by firework displays and entertainments by such popular figures as Elsie and Doris Waters ('Gert and Daisy'). The slump was on and many of the Manor Homes were occupied by men from Tyneside and other parts of the north, who had come south to seek work in the expanding London area. Other occupants moved out from places like Acton to find affordable houses, attracted by advertisements extolling Ruislip in terms more appropriate to Skegness – 'Live in Ruislip! The air's like wine. It's less than half an hour on the Piccadilly Line!'

A.J.A. Taylor and Davis Estates were building in the southern part of Eastcote and South Ruislip. This flurry of activity made Ruislip-Northwood the fastest growing area in the country between 1930 and 1939, the population trebling from 16,000 to 47,000. It had become part of Metroland so lovingly described by John Betjeman.

146. Firework display on 30 July 1933 advertising the Manor Homes.

147. The estate office for George Ball's Manor Homes in 1932.

148. Seaton Road – George Ball's Manor Homes. The first two houses on the right retain the original Crittall windows.

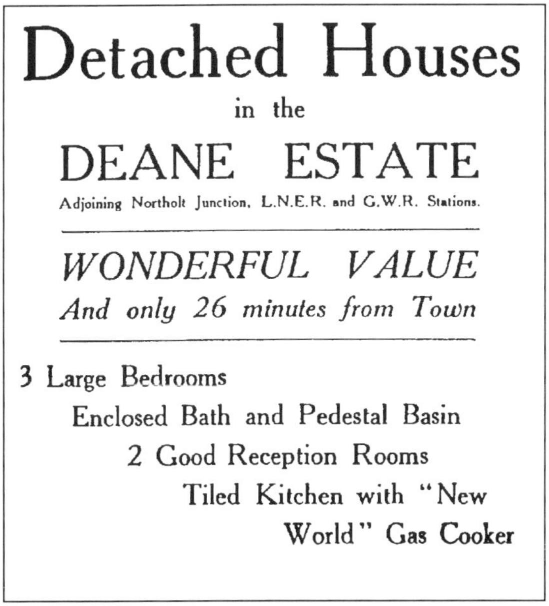

149. An advertisement for houses on the Deane Estate in 1932.

150. Bishop Winnington Ingram School 1931-68.

Schools – Ancient and Modern

RUISLIP NATIONAL SCHOOL

Continuous education has been available in Ruislip since 1812, when subscriptions were raised for a Charity School. The master, Thomas Gregory, who was also Vestry Clerk, and two mistresses, Mrs Seymour and Mrs Goulding, taught 50 pupils. In 1833 a school with 60 pupils taught by a master and a mistress received a National Society grant and later became Ruislip Church of England School. It flourishes today, though on a different site, as Bishop Winnington Ingram School.

RUISLIP CHURCH OF ENGLAND SCHOOL

A new school building and school house were erected by public subscription in 1864, in Eastcote Road on land given by King's College. A new headmaster,

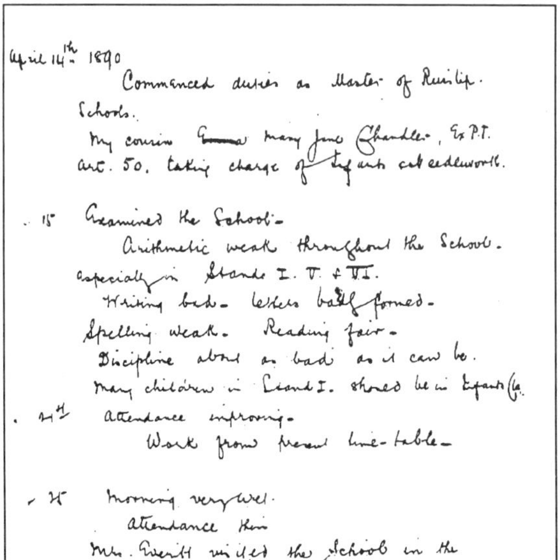

April 14th 1890
Commenced duties as Master of Ruislip Schools.
My cousin ~~Emma~~ Mary Jane Chandler, Ex P.T. Art. 50. taking charge of Infants and Needlework.

" 15 Examined the School.
Arithmetic weak throughout the School, especially in Stands I. V. & VI.
Writing bad – letters badly formed.
Spelling weak. Reading fair.
Discipline about as bad as it can be.
Many children in Stand I. should be in Infants Cl.

" 24 Attendance improving.
Work from present time-table.

" 25 Morning very wet.
Attendance thin
Mrs. Everitt visited the School in the afternoon & inspected the Needlework

" 28 School opened 9 a.m.
Attendance better than ever

151. A page from the log books of the Church of England school.

W.J. Taylor, was commended by the Reverend W. Campbell, HM Inspector in 1876. 'This is a very good and useful country school. It is taught with judgment and energy and the results of the examinations are most satisfactory.' The curriculum then included singing, drawing, physical geography, grammar and mapping. There were pupil teachers and local ladies, such as Mrs Roumieu the curate's wife and Miss Baker of Haydon Hall, listened to reading and inspected needlework.

The Headteachers all had difficulty in securing good attendance at school, partly because of the poor roads and lack of protective clothing in bad weather. In February 1897 the log book records: 'A shockingly wet morning. It has poured with rain all night. Only 40 children arrived at school in a very wet condition. I do not think it wise to retain them, but have sent a note to the vicar asking for instructions. He replies "Send the children home as the floods are getting very high and the Eastcote children must be cut off". This I at once did.'

Another reason for absence apart from illness was that many of the children worked whenever the opportunity offered. They gathered acorns in the autumn and sold them to local farmers for their pigs, collected blackberries and mushrooms and helped with the haymaking. The bigger boys went beating game for shooting parties, which was well paid.

The school was getting extremely dilapidated by 1927 and would have been taken over by the Middlesex Education Committee, ceasing to be a church school, but a benefactor, Laura Sawbridge came to the rescue and a new building was opened on the same site in 1931, with its name changed to Bishop Winnington Ingram. The site was sold for building development in 1968 and the school moved to Southcote Rise.

HOLY TRINITY AND OTHER NORTHWOOD PRIMARY SCHOOLS

Lord Robert Grosvenor (later Baron Ebury) of Moor Park supported a small school in Rickmansworth Road from about 1848. He endowed Holy Trinity church which was opened in 1854 on the same piece of land and was largely responsible for a new school building and school house erected alongside the church in 1861.

The development of Northwood after the opening of the station in 1887 increased the population and the school was enlarged in 1892. By 1906 there were 233 pupils and some walked long distances from the Half Mile Lane end of the parish. As more schools opened the numbers fluctuated, but the school is still on the same site, with 240 pupils in 1990 and the original buildings are still in use.

Other schools included the Half Mile Lane Infants' School begun under the auspices of Emmanuel church in a mission hut in Half Mile Lane in 1895; this was closed in 1978 when the children were dispersed to Hillside Infant and Junior School (built 1975) or to the newly-built Frithwood School. Middlesex County Education Committee opened Pinner Road Council School in 1910 – this too was replaced by Hillside.

152. Lady Bankes School 1936, designed by Curtis & Burchett.

SCHOOLS FOUNDED BETWEEN 1914 AND 1939

Coteford, an infants' school was opened in the Eastcote Village Institute at the bottom of Fore Street in 1926 and a junior school was built alongside in 1950. Since 1982 the juniors have shared a site with Grangewood (opened in 1977 for physically and mentally-handicapped children) and pupils from St Michael's Special School in Joel Street were integrated with them. The infants moved into the old junior buildings and the village institute was demolished.

The newly developing areas badly needed schools. Bourne Primary School opened as South Ruislip Council School near South Ruislip Station in 1931 and moved into its present premises in Cedar Avenue in 1962.

George Ball built Lady Bankes School which opened in January 1936 for the Manor Homes, the school having started in the Victoria Hall, Linden Avenue in 1934. The building by W.T. Curtis and H.W. Burchett is a fine example of Middlesex County Council school building, in the modernist style with a stair tower and octagonal roof lantern. It is now a listed building.

The Sacred Heart School opened in 1937 in Herlwyn Avenue to serve the Roman Catholic community. It has been rebuilt in stages and nothing now remains of the original building. The latest addition was blessed by Cardinal Hume in June 1990.

Whiteheath School opened in the Wallis Memorial Hall at Ruislip Common Methodist church in 1938 and moved to a new site at Whiteheath in 1947. The infants moved into a separate site further along Ladygate Lane in 1979.

Ruislip Gardens School opened in June 1940, having been delayed by the outbreak of war. The separate infants' and junior schools continue in the original buildings which have been relatively unchanged externally.

Another school that opened during the war was Deanesfield in January 1944, for the children of the Victoria Park estate in South Ruislip – Queen's Walk, Diamond Road, Jubilee Drive, Royal Crescent and Palace Way.

POST-WAR SCHOOLS

Field End Junior School opened in 1947, followed by an infants' section four years later, and Newnham in 1952. Field End Junior was regarded as a show case for modern school buildings and progressive education and visitors from Czechoslovakia, America, Denmark and Sweden came to study its teaching methods.

A second Roman Catholic school, Blessed (later Saint) Swithun Wells began in 1962 prior to the South Ruislip RC church of St Gregory being opened.

153. Field End Junior School, opened in 1947, the 'wonder school' of the NW Middlesex Education Committee.

154. St Helen's School, Northwood, was opened in 1899 by May Rowland-Brown, one of many private schools founded throughout the area as soon as the professional classes started to arrive. More than thirty which flourished between the wars, usually in ordinary houses, have now vanished.

SECONDARY EDUCATION

Manor School opened in 1926 on Eastcote Road and became a Church of England Comprehensive in 1977 with a new name, Bishop Ramsey. Northwood School in Potter Street, opened in 1934, also became a Comprehensive in 1977.

Queensmead School was planned as a Secondary Modern school in 1953. It was viewed as a 'school of the future' and advanced ideas of sound proofing, including double glazing were introduced because of its proximity to Northolt Airport.

St Nicholas Grammar School for Boys in 1955 and two years later St Mary's Grammar School for Girls opened on adjacent sites at the top of Wiltshire Lane. They were named after King's College, whose full title is the King's College of St Mary & St Nicholas. In 1977 they amalgamated to became Haydon School with a comprehensive intake.

Churches and Chapels for the new Suburbs

ST MARTIN'S PARISH IN MODERN TIMES

The mother parish now covers a greatly reduced area, three square miles instead of the original twelve, but within its circumscribed bounds, serves 22,000 souls (by no means all churchgoers), a hundredfold increase over the inhabitants of the far flung parish cared for by those nameless priests of the 11th century.

HOLY TRINITY

Lord Robert Grosvenor, later Baron Ebury of Moor Park, gave a site and £1000 towards the building costs of a church for Northwood. S.S. Teulon, the well-regarded Victorian church architect, designed Holy Trinity in an Early English style with a nave and chancel, using flint as his main material. It was conse-

RT. HON. LORD ROBERT GROSVENOR, 1st Baron Ebury. Born 24th April, 1801, died 19th November, 1893.

156. Lord Robert Grosvenor, who founded Holy Trinity Church.

155. Holy Trinity Church opened in 1854: S.S. Teulon was the architect. The north aisle was added in the same Early English style in 1895, and the south aisle and extension at the west end dates from 1927, and is by W. Charles Waymouth.

157. *The Hon. Victoria Grosvenor.*

crated on 14 January 1854, the ceremony nearly having had to be cancelled because of a blizzard which blocked the roads.

Some of the church windows are of interest. One with two angel figures on it was designed by Edward Burne-Jones in 1887 and commemorates Thomas George Grosvenor who died at St Petersburg in 1886 and was brought back to Northwood for burial. There are several Grosvenor family graves in the churchyard. A north aisle was added in 1895 to accommodate the increasing population. The Hon Victoria Grosvenor and her sister Albertine took a keen interest in the proceedings and helped the workmen by carrying flints in their donkey cart. Lady Victoria played the organ and trained the choir as well. A south aisle and baptistry were added in 1928 in a completely different Art Nouveau style, as yet more seating was required. By that time the parish of Northwood, like Ruislip before it had been subdivided.

158. *Emmanuel church, designed by Frank Elgood 1906.*

EMMANUEL CHURCH

The vicar of Holy Trinity opened a Church Mission Hut (known as the iron church) in Half Mile Lane in 1895 but by 1903 enough money had been raised to start work on a permanent red brick church, designed by Mr (later Sir) Frank Elgood, a member of Ruislip Parish Council and a well-known London architect. The church opened in 1904 and was consecrated in 1908, although the vestry, apse and spire were added later. It is now a thriving evangelical church and was further enlarged in the 1980s.

CHURCHES FOR A GROWING PLACE

The building of houses began close to the new Northwood Hills Station in 1934 and services were held in a tent on the site of the present St Edmund's church from September 1935. A dual-purpose hall was opened at the end of that year. St Edmund's, instituted as a parish in 1952 from parts of adjacent parishes, lies mostly in Pinner, and the present building was designed by Chachmaille Day between 1964 and 1968.

A temporary corrugated iron church was opened in Eastcote in December 1920 and dedicated to St Lawrence. Much of the money for the permanent building, opened in 1933 to the designs of Sir Charles Nicholson, was raised by Mr and Mrs Kenneth Goschen of Sigers, who held fêtes in their gardens; he was a governor of the Bank of England.

Building operations south of the railway line progressed from 1933 onwards and George Ball, the developer had agreed to build a church. St Paul's, Ruislip Manor, with its elegant interior opened in 1936.

South Ruislip was left churchless until 1931 when a wooden hall was used for services, but the present church of St Mary in the Fairway opened in 1959. The architect, Laurence Edward King was responsible for a number of churches in new suburban areas. A huge modern figure of Christ crucified on the outside of the tall full width west window is a striking feature.

159. *St Paul's, Ruislip Manor Church, opened in 1936.*

METHODISM

The seeds of Methodism sown by Adam Clarke at Haydon Hall in 1827 took root and a chapel was opened at the bottom of Field End Road (henceforth known as Chapel Hill) in 1848. The congregation was always large and lively and outgrew the chapel in the 1920s. A site on the opposite side of the road was bought and work was about to begin in 1939, just as war broke out. It was not until October 1960 that the new church, designed by George Baines & Syborn, was opened.

A small chapel was built at Ruislip Common in 1852 for Protestant Evangelical Dissenters, but the Primitive Methodists took it over in 1882. This was closed in 1994 and a query hangs over its future as a building.

There were also two Methodist churches in Northwood. The Primitive Methodists began at the corner of Half Mile Lane (later called the High Street) and Hallowell Road in 1896 and built a permanent church there in 1903. The Wesleyan Methodists' tin tabernacle was also in Hallowell Road, but they moved to a fine stone-built church in Oaklands Gate in 1924,

160. *Eastcote Methodist Chapel, Field End Road, opened May 1848 and demolished in 1962.*

161. The Primitive Methodist Church on the corner of Hallowell Road and Northwood High Street, built in 1896. It was a Synagogue for some years after 1965. The photograph shows it during demolition in 1981.

162. The Sacred Heart Church, founded by Eleanor Warrender, on Ruislip High Street in 1921.

which is where the two groups, united in 1965 still meet.

Ruislip Methodist church opened in 1923, services having previously been held at the Poplars. The original building is now the hall to a new church by George Baines and Syborn, opened in 1963. Members of the Ickenham Road church started meetings in one of George Ball's workmen's huts in 1934 and the Ruislip Manor church was built in 1937. A new church was erected alongside in 1978. South Ruislip Methodist Society was formed in the 1940s and the first church was built in 1950. A new one designed by Mauger, Gavin & Associates opened in 1964, but is now in a bad state of repair.

ROMAN CATHOLICISM

The first post-Reformation Catholic church was founded by Eleanor Warrender of Highgrove in 1921, dedicated to the Most Sacred Heart. It was built in the High Street. By 1939 land values had increased so much that the diocesan authorities sold the site and were able to build and pay for a new church in Pembroke Road and settle the debt on the Sacred Heart School. The new building designed by George Drysdale was nearer to the expanding Ruislip Manor.

St Thomas More's in Field End Road Eastcote was built in 1937 and continued to be a chapel-of-ease to Ruislip until 1950. Mass had earlier been said at The Grail, the former Field End House Farm. A new church was built in 1967 in a post-Vatican II style and the old church is now the hall.

Mass was first said in South Ruislip in the lounge of the Deane Arms. In 1958 a mass centre was opened in Queen's Walk by Father Philip Dayer. St Swithun Wells School opened in 1961 and was used for mass until a new church, St Gregory-the-Great's was ready in 1966.

St Matthew's, Northwood was financed by the Reverend Reginald B. Fellows, the first priest, who was a convert and former stockbroker. He transformed a former barn and stable in Hallowell Road in 1923 and a permanent church designed by W. Louis Carr was opened in June 1924.

OTHER PLACES OF WORSHIP

The Lutherans built St Andrew's in Whitby Road in 1967. Baptists started in Ruislip Manor in 1937 and the present church, by John Ainsworth, opened in 1964. There are Evangelical churches in Deane Avenue, South Ruislip (permanent church 1950) and Northwood Hills where a temporary church was started in 1951, a permanent church in 1961 and a larger building to accommodate increasing congregations in 1992. A Gospel Hall opened in Westway in 1935 and is now the Westway Chapel. There are two United Reformed churches, one in Northwood Hills and the other, St John's in Hallowell Road, began life in 1905 as a Presbyterian church. The permanent church which is still in use was completed during the First World War. The iron church which preceded it and the new church were both used as a VAD Hospital during the war. There is a Synagogue at Oaklands Gate and another in Shenley Avenue, Ruislip.

Saving Ruislip's Heritage

SQUATTERS AND ANCIENTS

Professional and business people moved into King's End and the Ruislip Park estate before the First World War. They were greeted with friendly mockery, soon being known as 'squatters' and retaliated by dubbing the original inhabitants 'ancients'. Often the newcomers were not particularly well off, but felt that they had a position to keep up. Mrs Mansford at Walden, for example, took in a lodger in order to be able to pay for a maid! These squatters grew to love the 'village atmosphere' (which of course their very presence was beginning to dispel) even though they disliked the mud in the High Street around the entrance to Wilkins Farm, which meant that they had to leave pairs of wellingtons at the station when they travelled to Town.

New estates were being planned in accordance with the Town Planning Scheme and parts of Copse Wood had already been cut down and the road which was to become Park Avenue had been driven through the bottom part of Park Wood. It would only be a matter of time before most of the woods had been built over and Manor Farm and the end of the High Street would have been redeveloped. The new residents became alarmed and began to speak of 'conservation' at meetings of the Ruislip Association.

SAVING THE WOODS AND MANOR FARM

Throughout 1929, discussions took place within the Association about the need to preserve the village centre around the church and the desirablity of having Park Wood maintained as a public open space. A Mr Menzies of the Royal Society of Arts was invited to visit Ruislip in January 1930 to point out those buildings most worthy of preservation. He chose Manor Farm, the Great Barn and Little Barn, the Old Post Office (now Village Tea Rooms and Duck Restaurant), the Old Bell (now RSPCA) and the Priest's House (now Barzolozzi's Restaurant).

163. The Earl of Crawford and Balcarres declaring Park Wood open to the public on the 23 July 1932. Perched on the edge of the platform beside him is Maynard Keynes, Bursar of King's College. Seated in the centre is E.R. Abbott, Clerk to the Council, and on his right, Mr Hutt, Chairman of RNUDC.

164. 'Granny' Tobutt, who lived at the Almshouses, Ruislip's oldest inhabitant, planting a commemorative tree in Park Wood, assisted by the Revd. Edward Cornwall Jones, vicar 1923-38.

165. Dr George Rylands of King's College addressing the crowd in Park Wood on 24 July 1982 – Ruislip Jubilee Day – to commemorate the 50th anniversary of the opening of Park Wood. The Mayor and Mayoress of Hillingdon, Councillor and Mrs Briggs sit on the left; Leonard Krause and Mrs Eileen Bowlt of RNELHS are on the right.

In November 1930 Mr J. Hooper of the Ruislip Association and the vicar, the Reverend Edward Cornwall-Jones were invited to attend the Audit Dinner at King's College, where they spoke at length with the Bursar, J. Maynard Keynes about the state of the woods and future plans. The College was amenable to the idea of Park Wood becoming a public open space and would have liked to end their 500-year-old association with Ruislip with a 'gracious act', by giving Park Wood, Manor Farm and the Old Post Office to the Ruislip-Northwood Urban District Council. However, the College was governed by the Universities' and Colleges' Act and considered as a trustee of its lands, so a sale had to be negotiated.

The final agreement reached in February 1931 was that Park Wood would be sold for £27,000 and Manor Farm and the Old Post Office would be included as a gift. Middlesex County Council was persuaded to contribute 75% of the cost on the grounds that the woods were used by many outsiders and railway trippers ('Visit Ruislip Woods in Bluebell time!' exhorted the Metropolitan Railway adverts) and Ruislip-Northwood Urban District Council agreed to put up the rest and maintain the woods as an open space. The southern part of the wood where building preparations had already begun were exempted from the sale and Broadwood Avenue, Sherwood Avenue, Park Avenue and cul-de-sacs off were developed in the years which followed.

Park Wood was declared open on 23rd July 1932 by the Earl of Crawford and Balcarres, chairman of the Council for the Preservation of Rural England; Mr Maynard Keynes was present and later at a tea in the Great Barn he was presented by Mrs Smedley with a commemorative parchment. Five trees were planted to mark the occasion, one by Mrs Tobutt, the oldest inhabitant (she lived to be over a hundred).

The *Advertiser and Gazette* waxed lyrical: 'The woodland scene was a fitting prelude when the great chief of the ardent band that seeks to retain our Ruritania was there to declare this Ancient Fairyland is to be retained by the people for ever'. The tea was followed by 'Rustic games and harmony on the lawn of the Manor House' and a massed camp fire and community singing ended the evening.

166. The exterior of the Little Barn at Manor Farm, imaginatively converted into a public library and opened by Professor Clapham, the Vice-Provost of King's College in November 1937.

167. *The interior of the public library housed in the converted Little Barn. Oak shelving, oak tables, rush-bottomed chairs and lantern-style lights were specially designed to be in keeping with the atmosphere of the barn.*

168. The Manor Farm rickyard seen across the horse pond when a unit of the Territorial Army were swimming in it during the First World War.

COPSE WOOD AND MAD BESS WOOD

All the speakers at the ceremony in 1932 assumed that what was left of Copse Wood and Mad Bess Wood was soon to be built over, but new ideas about the need for a green belt around London were gaining ground. The southern section of Copse Wood – 155 acres – was bought in conjunction with the Middlesex County Council and London County Council for £23,250 in 1936. Mad Bess Wood, consisting of 186 acres, were acquired by compulsory purchase from Sir Howard Stransom Button for £28,000 in the same year.

MANOR FARM

Richard Ewer left Ruislip as there was no longer land to farm and the Manor Farm buildings were gradually brought into public use. The house became a meeting place, the cowshed the Guide Hut and the stables a Boys' Club. The Little Barn was converted into a superb public library and opened by Professor J.H. Clapham, Vice-Provost of King's College on 2nd November 1937. The cow byre was used by the Horticultural Society until it was burnt down by arsonists in 1976. It was rebuilt as an exhibition room in 1980 and an archaeological dig during the rebuilding uncovered flints and wooden stakes from a much earlier building, perhaps the Abbey of Bec's Guest House. The Great Barn has been used for major exhibitions, jumble sales, craft fairs, archery and dog training.

The Winston Churchill Hall was built on the former Barn Close in 1965. Councillor T.R. Parker had purchased the land from King's College in 1932 and conveyed what became known as 'Parker's Piece' to the Ruislip Village Trust to be the site of a public hall and the Trust gave it to the Ruislip-Northwood Urban District Council in 1964, on condition that it would be used for no other purpose.

THE RUISLIP VILLAGE TRUST

The Ruislip Village Trust, a limited company, was set up in 1931 to buy the dilapidated timber-framed cottages next to the Police Station and backing onto the churchyard. In the late 1950s they ceased to be let as cottages and because of their condition were again in danger of demolition. Instead they were renovated in 1962 and converted into offices. The former gardens were flagged over and the pump was moved there in 1982.

169. The cottages which were acquired by the Ruislip Village Trust in 1931.

COTTAGES AND FARMHOUSES

The rest of Ruislip's heritage has not fared quite so well. Of the 135 houses mentioned in the Terrier of 1565 only 43 are still standing, but 16 others have disappeared since 1930 and some, Woodman Farm in Bury Street and Hill Farm in Orchard Close, for example, are now so closely surrounded by recently built houses (1980s and 90s) as to be almost impossible to see. The destruction of the environment of old houses and the loss of barns and other outbuildings rather than demolition is the threat of the 1990s to Ruislip's heritage.

Although most of its old buildings remain, Eastcote High Road has changed its character since losing Tapping's smithy and the building of Acacia Walk and the Black Horse Parade of shops in the early 1960s. Several farms and cottages have disappeared in Fore Street, Joel Street and Field End Road and the others are increasingly swamped by a few new houses built in former gardens, year by year.

In many ways Northwood suffered more from infilling and redevelopment in the 1970s and 80s than the other parts of the ancient parish, partly because the late Victorian and Edwardian builders created large squares of adjoining gardens, making possible the insertion of new estates.

170. Eastcote High Road, probably about 1910. Teas are being provided at the timber-framed Old Barn House and at one of the small cottages. The gap between the Old Barn House and the cottages had only recently been filled and the Bensons ran the Post Office there.

TEAS
PROVIDED

However, the saving of the woods, Manor Farm and the High Street cottages were the most important events in Ruislip's metamorphosis into a suburb, ensuring that it retains some continuity with its rural past and has a recreational area just about large enough to get out of earshot of modern traffic. The events of 1929-32 were a triumph.

171. Fore Street Farm was the home of the Powell family from the 1870s. Ralph Hawtrey Deane sold it to Standard Estates for development in 1933.

172. The Homestead in Wiltshire Lane was demolished in 1958 by the Andersons of Eastcote Place, who built nine bungalows in its place.

173. Ramin on Eastcote High Road has a jettied late 16th-century extension built onto a slightly earlier house. Two later cottages adjoin it, making one large house.

174. Tapping's Smithy closed in 1958 and the Smithy cottage on the right was demolished the following year.

175. The Grange in Eastcote High Road is a long weatherboarded building which used to be a separate house and barn dating from the 16th century. The two were joined in the 1920s by Mr and Mrs C.N.G. Dore. The cottage on the left of the picture was once a stable and coach house. The barn seen in the centre is now offices.

176. Ruislip Reservoir in the 1920s

Ruislip Lido

THE RESERVOIR

Ruislip Reservoir was created in 1811 to be a feeder for the Grand Junction Canal. The site chosen was a shallow valley with a stream running through; Park Wood came down to the water's edge on the south and the cottages of the old hamlet of Park Hearne stood on rising ground to the north; the rest of the land was common waste. At the time of the enclosures (1804-14) portions of common were sold to help cover administrative costs.

The Grand Junction Canal Company purchased nearly 56 acres from the commissioners and 61½ acres of Park Wood from King's College and the cottages and gardens, amounting to 35 acres, from various owners. There was some opposition from Henry Golder the only owner/occupier who at first refused to treat with the company on any terms, but negotiations were completed in August 1807. For a few years the land was let and some of the cottages may have continued to be inhabited, as there is a story that the Militia from Windsor was called out to evict residents when the time came to demolish them. A few years later new cottages were built on the south side of the newly laid out Reservoir Road.

Construction began in 1811, John Rennie being the consulting engineer and Hugh Mackintosh the constructor. On 5th December 1811 Rennie reported to the General Meeting of the Committee of Management of the Grand Junction Waterworks Company, 'The Reservoir at Ruislip has now been completed and although doubts were entertained with respect to its capability of being filled with water owing to an extensive bed of sand which was found near to its head, yet this has answered the most sanguine wishes as it is now nearly full of water and from the latest accounts transmitted to me there is no appearance of any leakage in it.'

Remnants of the Park Hearne cottages and of the strip of Park Wood occasionally surface. When the water was drained in 1990 a rectangular 'crop mark', 13 feet by 9 feet in size, of darker damp mud was noted. Careful probing with a trowel uncovered a crumbling brick wall more than 12 inches high, covered in grey-black silt. The position seemed to correspond to the most northerly of the dwellings shown on the enclosure map, a cottage owned by John Dean. Stumps of oak trees were exposed on the site of Park

177. Ruislip Lido

Wood, close together at a density of about 300 to the acre, which left no room for hornbeam underwood and suggests that the oaks themselves were coppiced in that part of the wood, possibly to supply bark for tanning.

THE FEEDER

The Grand Junction Canal Company was empowered to supply piped water from the canal to the inhabitants of Paddington in 1798. An Act of Parliament of 1811 transferred these powers to the Grand Junction Waterworks Company which undertook the works at Ruislip and in February 1813 the company resolved to make a feeder to connect the reservoir with the canal. The route chosen, to enter the canal near Hayes Bridge, was between seven and eight miles long; the water ran in the feeder for the first time on 4 June 1816, according to an entry in the diary of James Ewer of Hill Farm. It was entirely man-made and did not make use of any natural waterways because of objections from millers who did not want water to be deflected from the River Colne which was fed by the streams.

The feeder was not a success – it collected drainage and flood waters from the lands on either side of it and contaminated both the canal and Paddington's water supply. An extension was constructed in 1817 from Hayes Bridge to the Brentford Arm to avoid pollution of the Paddington Arm.

The reservoir itself was not entirely successful either, being rather shallow in comparison with its surface area and was not used to supply water to the canal after 1851. In 1891 gamekeepers were appointed for 'Ruislip Reservoir and the banks thereof.... to preserve the game.... and seize all such guns, dogs, ferrets, nets or engines for killing and taking conies, hare, rabbits, pheasant or other game....'

RUISLIP LIDO

The reservoir was used for both skating and swimming in the 1920s and the Grand Union Canal Company, with which the Grand Junction amalgamated in 1933, began to develop the area as a Lido, with boating, fishing and swimming facilites. A white central building with flanking wings, by George W. Smith, very much in the modern style was built in 1936 and a terrace and curved concrete swimming pool lay in front.

After the nationalisation of British Waterways the Lido came under the aegis of the British Transport Commission, from whom it was purchased in 1951 by the Ruislip-Northwood Urban District Council. Ruislip Yacht Club had its headquarters in the grounds and water-skiing championships were sometimes held there. Since the draining of the Lido in 1990 the water level has been kept artificially low for fear of

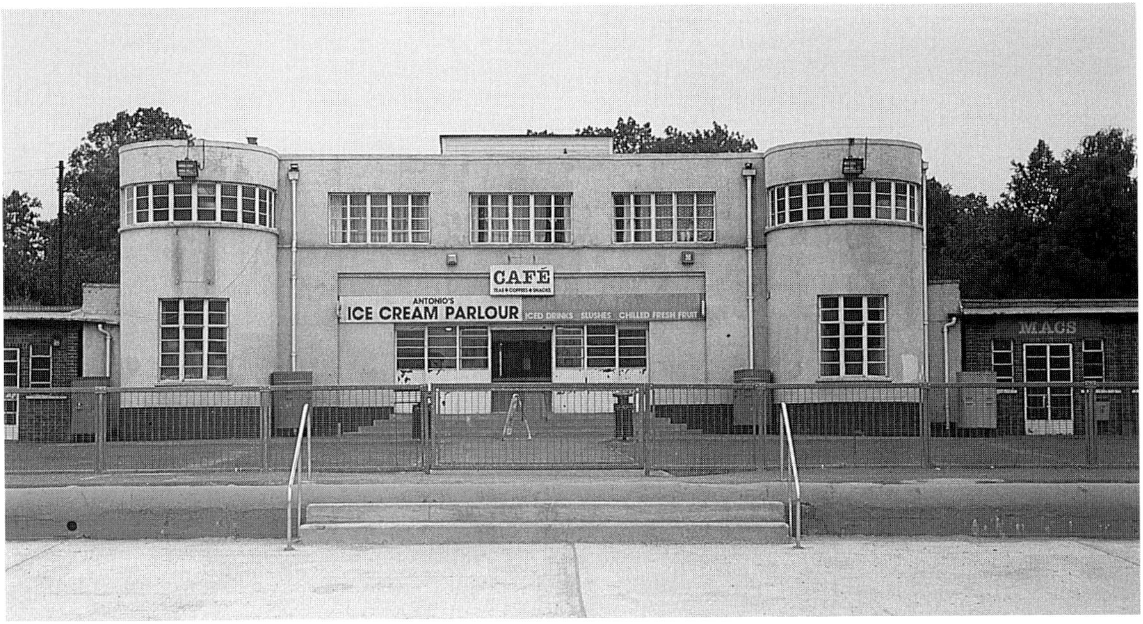

178. The modern Lido buildings designed by George W. Smith.

179. The opening of the Lido by the Earl of Howe in May 1936.

flooding houses built on the bed of the old feeder in the 1970s. After some years of neglect and vandalism the Lido building was damaged by fire in June 1993 and was demolished in March 1994.

180. The Lido in winter. Skating and ice-hockey in 1946.

181. Boats at the Lido.

182. A Dakota which failed to take off from Northolt landed on the roofs of 44 and 46 Angus Drive on 19 December 1946 (see page 132)

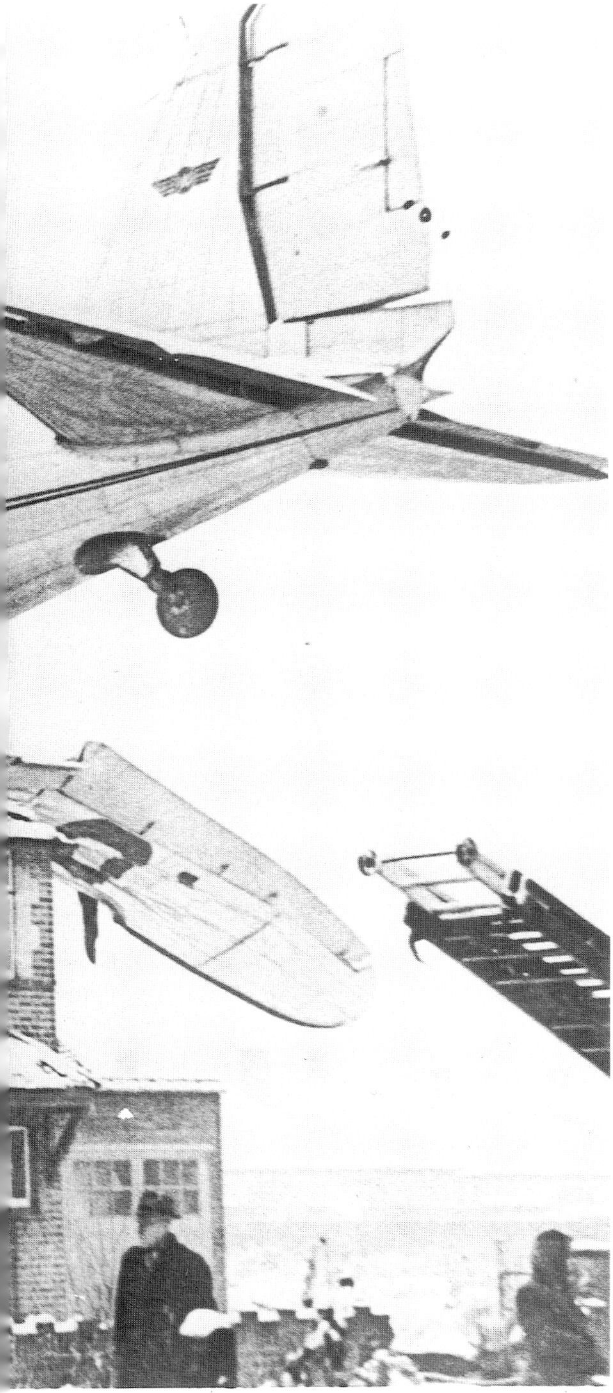

Northolt Aerodrome

The land in South Ruislip which had once been the common fields of Ruislip proved very attractive to early aviators, being open, fairly flat, well drained and with rail connections with central London. Priors Farm was under consideration for Harrow Aerodrome in 1912, when an airfield with thirty hangars and sports facilities was being contemplated. Claude Graham-White lived at the White House (formerly the Laurels) in Sharps Lane while looking for suitable fields in the locality, but he chose land in Hendon and opened an aerodrome there instead.

The outbreak of war in 1914 increased the need for places where men of the Royal Flying Corps could receive instruction. A Major Brancker, Deputy Director of Military Aeronautics at the War Office, ordered land in South Ruislip to be requisitioned for Northolt Aerodrome, but there is some doubt as to which land the Major had in mind, as there has long been a story that the official who came to Ruislip held his map upside down and took Glebe Farm, Hundred Acres and part of Down Barnes Farm by mistake. The new airfield soon extended west to take over part of Hill Farm in Ickenham parish. The name of the aerodrome came from the nearest station, Northolt Junction (now South Ruislip).

The aerodrome, consisting mostly of wooden-framed hangars covered in canvas, was officially opened on 3 March 1915. A group of White Russians and Americans were trained there along with the British airmen. Throughout the war there were many accidents during training, some fatal; 16 men were killed during 1917. Military funerals, the coffins draped with a flag, winding their way up West End Road to St Martin's were an intriguing sight for Ruislip's children who stood by the station bridge to watch.

Small boys soon became adept at recognising the different types of planes. The Avro 504 was the basic trainer, but there were also Shorthornes, Morane Monoplanes, Henry Farman's BE2Cs and many others. When they came down in hedgerows they were quickly stripped by souvenir hunters and the Commanding Officer demanded better police protection of government property after valuable instruments disappeared from a blood-stained Sopwith Camel, whose pilot had been taken to hospital from a field close to Ruislip Manor Station early in 1918.

Between the wars the airfield was used for testing new aircraft by Fairey Aviation, Martin Baker and others, but military activity fluctuated.

183. The entrance to the Aerodrome from Western Avenue, with a Spitfire as a reminder of the Battle of Britain.

THE BATTLE OF BRITAIN

Northolt was a fighter station during the Second World War and played an important part in the Battle of Britain in 1940. It was remarkable for the presence there of numerous Polish and Canadian airmen and after the war the Polish War Memorial, a famous landmark on the Western Avenue, designed by Miecystam Lubelski, was erected to commemorate Polish men lost in the war. Group Captain Stanley Vincent was in command throughout the Battle of Britain. It was his idea to camouflage the hangars by painting them like rows of suburban houses and marking out apparent gardens and a meandering stream on the main runway.

A CIVIL AERODROME

After the war civil aircraft increasingly used Northolt for European flights, particularly those of British European Airways – Bealine House, a very plain office block, was built in 1964, but was replaced by the friendlier looking Sainsbury's in 1987. Northolt was later used by Aer Lingus, Swissair, Alitalia and other airlines and soon facilities became inadequate. Two daily London-Paris flights moved to Heathrow in 1950 and gradually the others followed. The last BEA flight flew out of Northolt in October 1954.

'DAKOTA REST'

Number 46 Angus Drive, South Ruislip is called 'Dakota Rest' and many people must wonder why. It is because a Dakota crash-landed on the roofs of numbers 44 and 46 on 19th December 1946 – an event caught dramatically in the picture on page 130. The BEA plane had tried to take off from Northolt in the middle of a bad snowstorm and snow freezing onto the fuselage prevented it from gaining height. Passengers and crew climbed out onto the roof of number 46, through the skylight into the loft and emerged through the front door. Mrs Zigmond was at her gate next door, buying fish and the fishmonger raced into the house to snatch her sleeping baby son as the plane roared overhead. The Levines had not yet moved into number 46 as they were due to be married in a couple of days time, but their furniture and wedding presents already installed survived undamaged.

MILITARY AERODROME

Northolt retains its position as London's Military Aerodrome and is constantly in use by VIPs, its easy communication with London, nowadays via Western Avenue, making its position just as suitable now as in the early days of aviation for a small airfield near the capital. In the summer of 1994 it was expected that the Queen's Flight would be moved to Northolt from RAF Benson. The building of a new VIP lounge led to fears in the neighbourhood that civilian use of the aerodrome might rise to an unacceptably high level.

The War Years 1939-45

REQUISITIONING OF SCHOOLS AND LARGE HOUSES

Long before war broke out the government had been considering how best to prepare for the impending 'emergency'. The country was divided into areas designated as dangerous, neutral or safe. There was an assumption that on the outbreak of war, schoolchildren would be evacuated from dangerous places to reception centres in safe areas and that those in neutral zones would stay at home. Ruislip-Northwood was classed as neutral, but later, in June 1940, children living within 1000 yards of Northolt Aerodrome were advised to join the evacuees and trenches (shelters) were dug in school grounds.

Five schools were requisitioned in August 1939. That in Potter Street housed an ambulance station, stretcher bearers, ambulance drivers, a Red Cross mobile unit, nursing staff and a women's canteen committee. Lady Bankes had a First Aid Post and an

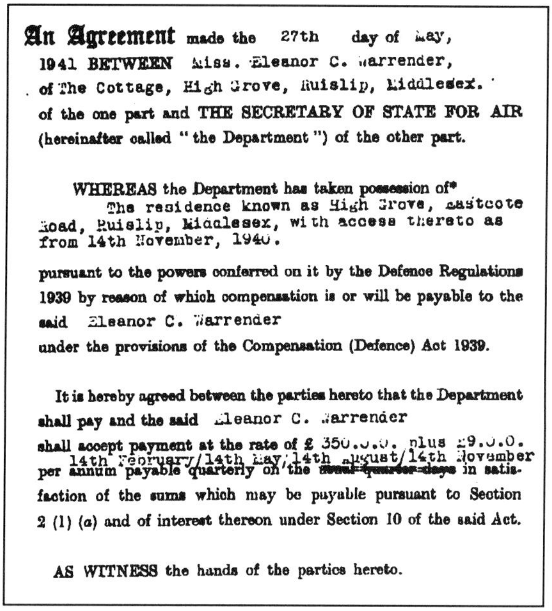

An Agreement made the 27th day of May, 1941 BETWEEN Miss. Eleanor C. Warrender, of The Cottage, High Grove, Ruislip, Middlesex. of the one part and THE SECRETARY OF STATE FOR AIR (hereinafter called "the Department") of the other part.

WHEREAS the Department has taken possession of* The residence known as High Grove, Eastcote Road, Ruislip, Middlesex, with access thereto as from 14th November, 1940.

pursuant to the powers conferred on it by the Defence Regulations 1939 by reason of which compensation is or will be payable to the said Eleanor C. Warrender under the provisions of the Compensation (Defence) Act 1939.

It is hereby agreed between the parties hereto that the Department shall pay and the said Eleanor C. Warrender shall accept payment at the rate of £ 350.0.0. plus £9.0.0. per annum payable quarterly on the ~~usual quarter-days~~ 14th February/14th May/14th August/14th November in satisfaction of the sums which may be payable pursuant to Section 2 (1) (*a*) and of interest thereon under Section 10 of the said Act.

AS WITNESS the hands of the parties hereto.

185. Extract from the requisition document for Haydon Hall.

184. Three local wardens photographed in February 1941, Messrs Poulter, Bursnall and Crouch, who were awarded the OBE.

186. Sandbags around Manor Farm during the war.

ambulance station in the school and an ARP post in the grounds and Manor Senior had an ambulance station.

Most of the great houses – the Grange, Haydon Hall and Highgrove were also taken over. Miss Warrender received £350 per annum and Haydon Hall was the ARP Report and Control Centre for a few months until an old bakery near the Oaklands Gate Council Offices was converted.

AIR RAIDS

Air raids started in August 1940 and continued until March 1941. Public buildings were surrounded by sand bags to protect them from blast and sirens were fixed to Ruislip and Northwood Police Stations. The most unusual shelter was built in the garden of 38 Sandy Lodge Way, Northwood by Egbert Shilacker in 1938. He had connections with the armaments industry and built a circular concrete structure about 10 feet in diameter and 10 feet high with a domed roof; the walls, roof and base were 10 inch thick sandwiches with armament steel plate in the middle and there were deep-set windows and a door which could be fitted with steel plates; a stove with an odd little chimney gave heat and water and electric light were laid on.

School children spent much of the day in their trenches. Most nights had their disturbances as well and an order was made that if the 'all clear' did not go until after midnight schools should not start until 10.30 in the morning. A survey of 338 Ruislip children's sleeping arrangements carried out in November 1940 disclosed that 5 slept in a bed upstairs, 171 slept downstairs, 79 were in Anderson shelters, 39 in garden shelters, 14 in public shelters and 30 were under the stairs.

There were many public shelters in the streets. These were damp and insanitary and St John's Ambulance members attended them to do all they could to prevent colds and treat minor ailments.

During 1940-1, 208 High Explosive bombs fell on Ruislip and Northwood, 1150 incendiary bombs, 28 shells, 3 parachute mines and a number of unexploded bombs and shells. 146 houses were demolished, 482

187. Bomb damage at Ruislip Manor.

severely damaged and 3239 were slightly damaged; 23 people were killed and 52 injured. There was scarcely any damage done in 1942 and 1943, but the flying bombs of 1944 destroyed another 17 houses and killed four more people.

The most serious loss of life was caused by a crippled Wellington bomber, unable to reach Northolt, which crash landed in Station Approach, South Ruislip on a Sunday afternoon in October 1942. It ended on its back in a field and the ammunition started going off as it caught fire: 21 people died including two sisters and their four children who were taking an afternoon stroll. A survivor, Richard Vennai remembers a man in the gun turret waving his hands at children playing in the field, warning them to get out of the way.

BRITISH RESTAURANTS AND FOOD PRODUCTION

British Restaurants were established in the area and launched by celebrities. The first, in Victoria Road, Ruislip Manor, was opened in October 1941 by Elsie and Doris Waters. Another followed in the converted Ritz Cinema in Northwood High Street where Freddie Grisewood did the honours in February 1942 and the author L.A.G. Strong opened the restaurant at Eastcote.

In an effort to provide sufficient food many residents cultivated allotments as well as former lawns in their gardens and the local horticultural societies flourished. Some open spaces like the Pinn Fields were cultivated and sheep were grazed on the golf courses.

BATTLE OF BRITAIN HOUSE

Josef Conn obtained a lease from King's College in 1905 of land called Ducks Hill Plantation and Horsens, which had once been part of Copse Wood. He built a handsome house with views across the Reservoir to Harrow church and even to Box Hill, and his Danish wife who was a physiotherapist treated her patients there. In 1920 Meyer Franklin Kline, an American Shipping Magnate, took over the lease and renamed the house 'Kokyo' (he had interests in the Far East) and later 'Franklin House' (after President Roosevelt). He improved the house by building in furniture from luxury cabins from his ships and strewed the grounds with eastern ornaments.

He was in America in 1939 and the house was let to a German who had to move out under defence regulations, whereupon the house was allocated to the United States Forces as Headquarters for a 'Clandestine Operations' Division and agents were trained there for sabotage operations in occupied Europe. It is said (but has not been confirmed) that General Eisenhower and Winston Churchill held secret meetings there.

After the war a war memorial scheme was set up to commemorate the Battle of Britain. The aim was to purchase the house, rename it Battle of Britain House and arrange various activities, including 'exchange visits of the youth of Britain and the Empire, living together under the same roof, fostering the community spirit and breeding solid friendships.' However, insufficient funds were raised and the Middlesex County Council bought the freehold from King's College and decided to use the house for the welfare of young people and the training of youth leaders. It opened in 1948, but the official opening ceremony was performed by Air Chief Marshal Sir James Robb on 1st March 1949. The badges of the squadrons involved in the Battle of Britain were fixed to the dining room panels.

It was run for many years by Victor Stanyon as a short term residential college, with many courses for children and adults and it became the field headquarters of the newly formed Ruislip & District Natural History Society in 1951. The house burnt down in August 1984, and many plans for the site, which the Council wished to sell off, were rejected or fell through; eventually, in 1993, the best of all possible solutions was found, when the Council agreed that the land should be taken back into the woodland from which it had been carved in 1905.

AMERICANS IN RUISLIP

United States troops were stationed in Ruislip after the war and a base was built on the land zoned for industry in South Ruislip. GIs became a familiar sight in the area and the George Inn, one of their meeting places, attracted ladies from London who came out on the Met. on Saturday evenings. The base was occupied until the 1970s and many trans-Atlantic marriages took place with local girls. The abiding memory of men who were then small boys, is of going around asking "Got any gum, chum?"

188. Franklin House was acquired as a memorial to those who fought in the Battle of Britain and opened to provide short courses in the liberal arts in 1948. It was afterwards known as Battle of Britain House.

189. Victory tea-party in Crosier Way 12 May 1945. A street shelter can be seen in the background.

Recent Years

THE KROGERS

The Cold War succeeded the Second World War and Ruislip hit the headlines in 1961 with the news that Helen and Peter Kroger, heavily involved in the Portland Spy case, had been living in Ruislip at 45 Cranley Drive. The Krogers settled in the bungalow and passed themselves off as New Zealanders, although both were from New York and had strong Bronx accents. Peter Kroger posed as an antiquarian bookseller and the couple made friends with their neighbours and took an interest in the local children. They were never, however, available for social engagements on Saturday evenings, which was the time that their colleague, Gordon Lonsdale ,visited them, walking to their bungalow along a footpath that led into the cul de sac.

When they finally fell under suspicion police kept surveillance from a neighbour's house, greatly to the distress of the family who were particularly fond of the Krogers and found the truth difficult to believe.

After their arrest a Ronson cigarette lighter was found to hold codes, an Ever-ready battery a KGB expense sheet and a tin of talcum powder was in fact a microdot reader. Helen Kroger's handbag contained a film of microdots with details of operations at Portland's naval research station. The radio transmitter was dug up from the garden only in 1977, despite an extensive police search at the time. The Krogers were jailed, but were exchanged for Gerald Brooke in 1969 and returned first to Warsaw and in 1972 to Russia. Helen Kroger died in 1993.

DEVELOPMENTS AFTER THE WAR

The Second World War marked the end of very rapid growth. Since then land zoned for industrial use has been developed as the South Ruislip Industrial Estate and the erection of a tall office block beside Ruislip Station in the early 1960s marked the beginning of a spate of office building near all the stations, which has changed the residential areas surrounding them. Only a small proportion of residents are employed locally. Many still work in London, but nowadays often drive rather than run to the station, while others are employed in Uxbridge, at Stockley Park and Heathrow.

The High Street shops in all parts of the district are in decline as supermarkets have been built away from the original shopping centres and smaller shopkeepers driven away by high rentals have been replaced by estate agents and eating places. There are 18 restaurants or fast food outlets on Ruislip High Street alone.

190. New shops in Ruislip High Street c1929, built on the grounds of The Poplars.

BAIRD

191. The Astoria on Ruislip High Street opened in September 1934, showing Catherine the Great. *It was given a crinkly steel front and a new name, the Embassy, in the 1970s.*

193. The Rivoli in Ickenham Road was closed to make way for Sainsbury's in 1966.

192. Ruislip High Street at the top of Midcroft, 1930s.

194. Ruislip High Street looking toward the station in the 1920s.

The cinemas, two in Ruislip, and one each in Northwood, Northwood Hills and Eastcote have all gone. The Rivoli was replaced by Sainsbury's in 1966, but that too has now closed down. The Job Centre stands where the Astoria (later the Embassy) used to be and there are offices on the site of Eastcote's Ideal cinema. The Northwood Hills Odeon stood where the Gateway Food Store is today and the small cinema in Northwood High Street is now an Old Folk's Dining Club.

Broadly speaking many of the ideas of the town planners had been brought into effect by 1960. Most of the streets were lined with trees and were arranged with corner houses on larger plots so that a spacious park-like atmosphere was created. Nearly every house had a garden of fairly generous proportions, enhancing this effect and the towers of the various churches rose above the roof tops of the surrounding houses. A garden suburb had come into existence which was better than the planners had intended because it retained some ancient features and most of the woodland.

195. The Northwood Hills Odeon cinema, built in 1933, the year that the station opened and development began. It later became the Rex.

INDEX

Pages with illustrations are marked with an asterisk.